Drawing ZENDOODLE

How to incorporate zendoodle into drawings of animals

By Irene Blount

Copyright©2015 Irene Blount

Table of Contents

Disclaimer

While all attempts have been made to verify the information provided in this book, the author does assume any responsibility for errors, omissions, or contrary interpretations of the subject matter contained within. The information provided in this book is for educational and entertainment purposes only. The reader is responsible for his or her own actions and the author does not accept any responsibilities for any liabilities or damages, real or perceived, resulting from the use of this information.

The trademarks that are used are without any consent, and the publication of the trademark is without permission or backing by the trademark owner. All trademarks and brands within this book are for clarifying purposes only and are the owned by the owners themselves, not affiliated with this document.

Introduction

The most effective method to Draw Fantasy Creatures

Drawing fantasy creatures like unicorns, mermaids, and dragons can at first be a troublesome thing to do and it takes some practice yet there are some fundamental standards you can take after to make marvelous creatures and make them look incredible.

Drawing fantasy creatures takes a few abilities that go past the ordinary domain of drawing on the grounds that you can't locate a subject to posture for you - unless you live in a captivated timberland! So you are confronted with not just the undertaking of learning how to draw you are additionally confronted with the test of taking advantage of your imagination and after that putting this down on paper. Here are some strong tips that will offer you some assistance with imagining and draw better fantasy creatures.

Instructions to Tap into your Imagination

1. Doodling and drawing with a free-form is the most ideal approach to get your creativity and imagination streaming. The procedure to take after is to just draw fast sketches and after that adjust them as things begin. It resembles the following: Draw a generally human molded head then begin

to add a body to it yet don't intentionally make it a human body, change your lines and see where it goes. You will be astounded by what happens. Your eye will begin to see things differently and you will make some incredible creatures. These ought to just be fast sketches and you ought to draw bunches of them - fill the sheet of paper and see where the drawings go. This is an incredible approach to think of the starting thought for another fantasy creature.

2. Changing the state of existing creatures and animals - Many of the most recognizable fantasy creatures are varieties of well known animals. A Unicorn is a variety of a steed and a Dragon is a variety of a Dinosaur. Consider different creatures and doodle their unpleasant shape while concocting varieties. What might a feline look like on the off chance that it had scales rather than hide? Alternately what about a Giraffe with short legs?

3. The Power of Combining Animals - this is an effective approach to make new fantasy creatures and Greek Mythology is stacked with this sort of monster. A Centaur is half man and half steed; and a mermaid is half woman and half fish. The conceivable outcomes are inestimable and when you are doodling out thoughts don't constrain yourself to simply upper and lower body blends. Take a

stab at consolidating appendages, middles, heads, hands, feet or whatever else that strikes you.

4. The inventive force of twisting - Often times fantasy creatures are twists of humans or different animals. Think about your drawing as a chunk of dirt that you can mold into any shape. Mutilate the arms, legs, middle, head or whatever else. This will harvest some extraordinary results. In the event that you draw a human that is exceptionally thin with a larger than usual head you are making a beeline for something troll like. What's more, in the event that you draw a human that is thick and stocky you may be making a beeline for a Troll or Ogre.

5. Here are two or three bizarre approaches to take advantage of your imagination and make irregular fantasy

creatures. Have a go at making an uncommon sound then attempt to draw the creature or monster that would make that sound. On the other hand work out a depiction in words for your mammoth then attempt to draw it. These two methods bring different parts of your mind into the procedure not only your dexterity.

1. Everything identifies with human life structures - If you work on drawing individuals you will show signs of improvement at drawing fantasy creatures. The same fundamental tenets of musculature and skeletal understructure apply to every single natural creature - even made up ones. Keep in mind: Skin or hide is something that covers muscles and bones however don't totally conceal it. The bones and muscles appear on the other side. So draw more individuals and your fantasy creatures will move forward.

2. Draw all the more existing creatures - Fantasy creatures are quite often varieties of creatures and animals that as of now exist. On the off chance that you need to draw a dragon you ought to consider and look at pictures of dinosaurs and huge reptiles. On the off chance that you need to draw a unicorn you ought to utilize a steed as your model. Furthermore, there are many minor departure from the human structure. In the event that you need to draw a diminutive person, a mythical person or a troll you can utilize the human structure as an impeccable beginning stage. The imperative thing to recall is that the more steeds you draw the better your unicorns will be and the more dinosaurs you draw the better your dragons will be. Also, the best thing about this is you can undoubtedly discover pictures of steeds and dinosaurs to look at while you draw.

3. Utilize you're drawing devices for more expression - When drawing a creature you need to think about its air. Is it a delicate creature or a mean creature? Utilize your pencil in a way that communicates this. Dim, bold and sharp lines are generally better when drawing furious or startling creatures and delicate lines are typically better for tender, legendary creatures. This is something that is frequently overlooked yet it is critical. You are utilizing your pencil as a part of a way that goes past simply drawing lines. Also, this applies to an entire range of systems including short lines, long lines, rough lines and notwithstanding shading.

4. Try not to falter to look at and duplicate different people groups work. Painstakingly looking at other fantasy work will enhance your work drastically. While doing a duplicate you are compelled to see things you wouldn't typically see and this is an incredible approach to learn how to do it

without anyone's help. - Just don't guarantee the creature as your own.

5. Keep a sketch and doodle book and work in it frequently. This is something that works genuine well for me in light of the fact that looking over many pages of doodles you have done in the past will regularly rouse new thoughts for drawings of creatures.

Many individuals have a powerful urge to learn how to draw animals practical, and on the off chance that you are one of those many individuals, you may be pondering what the most ideal approach to learn is. You can, obviously get craftsmanship guideline through a class or course, or you can procure a private teacher for individual, one-on-one lessons, as well. The most reasonable and advantageous approach to learn, however, is through getting a regulated instructional book.

Chapter 1 – How to draw a lion

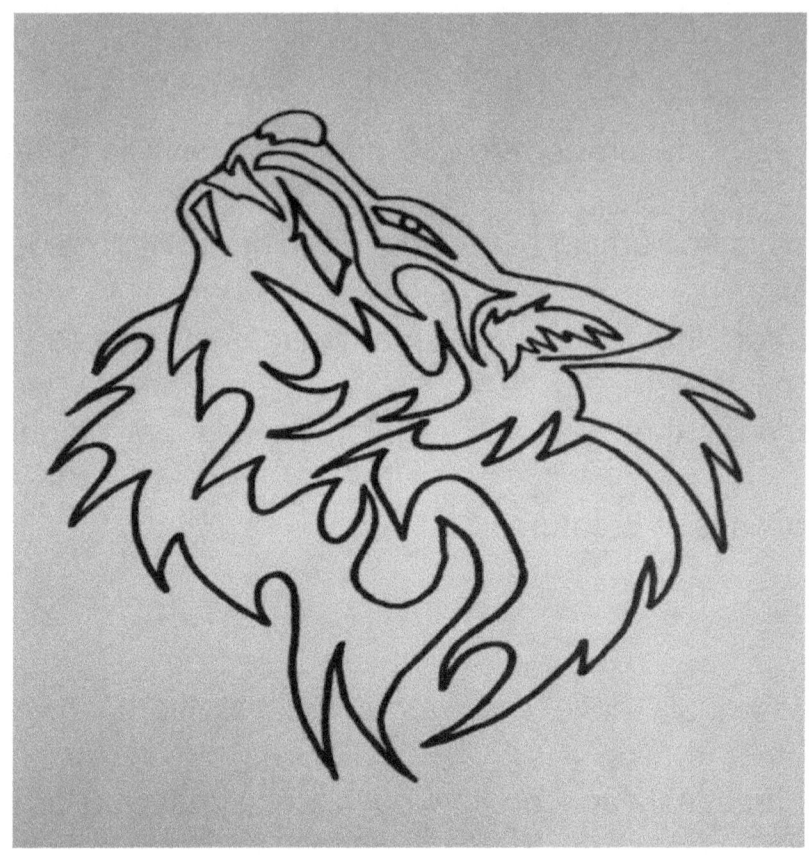

Step 1: Begin with a head shape, and after that draw out the lions, nose shape like you see here. Finally, draw a long line for the bended neck.

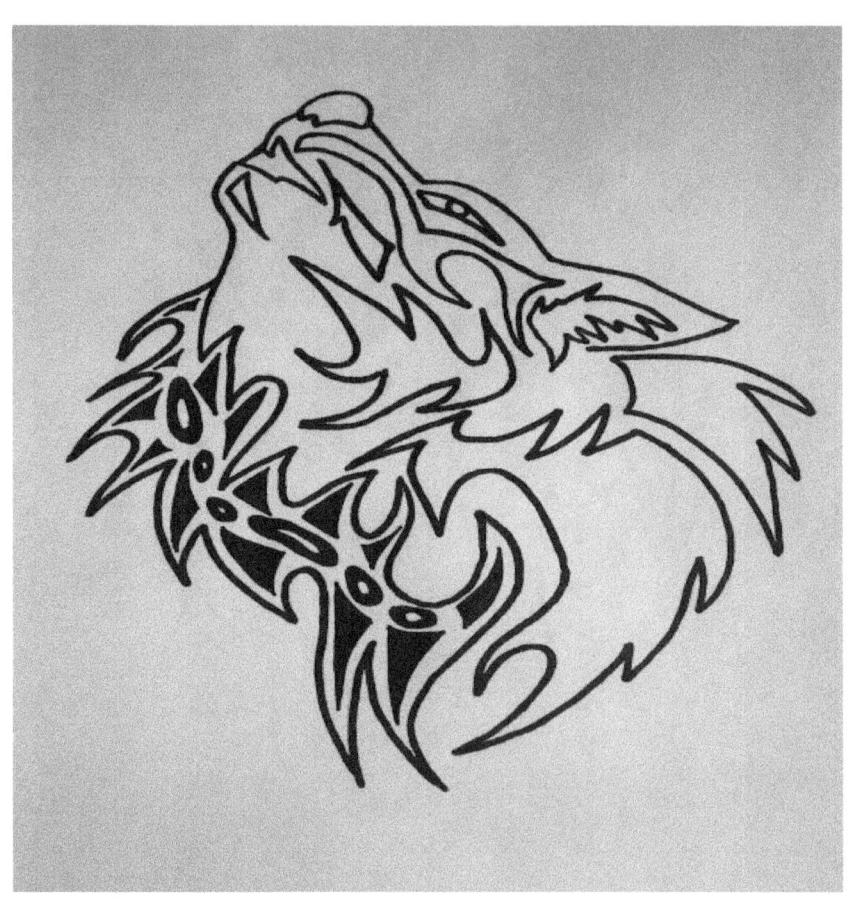

Step 2: Sketch out the nose, and afterward draw in the lion's mouth line. Next, draw the little eye, and after that begin the state of the ear. The ear ought to be somewhat bigger then that of a tiger.

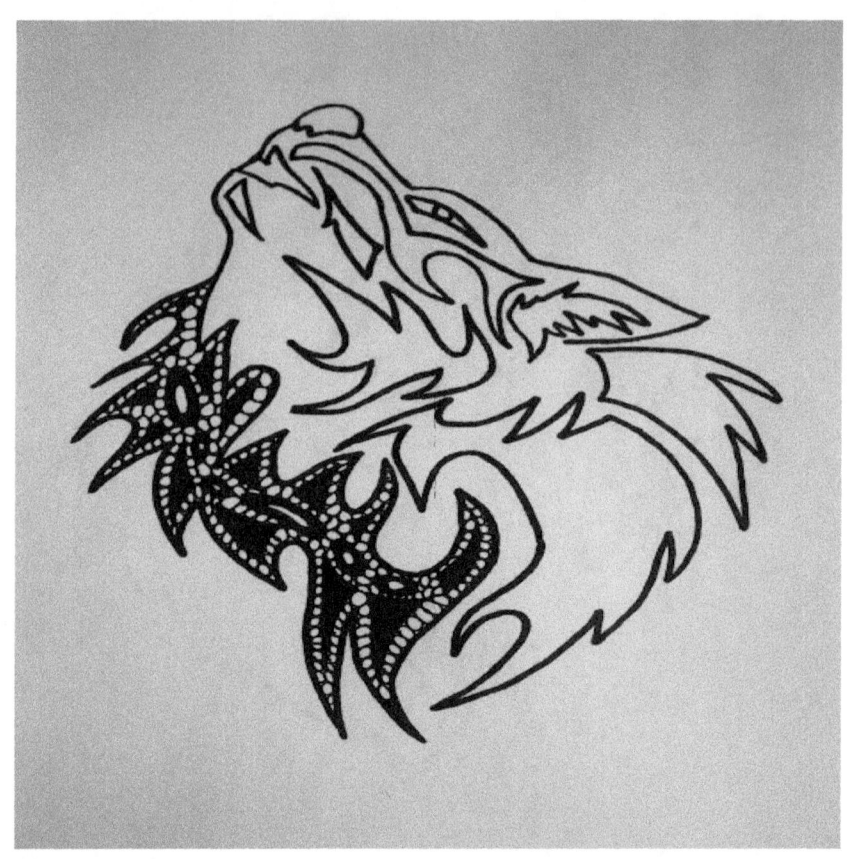

Step 3: Alright, here is the place you will begin sketching, and quit drawing. You should sketch out the rage jaw, neck or mane hair, and after that sketch in the brow, cheek, and detail within the lions ear like you see here. Include some wavy hair under the eye, and after that along the extension of the nose.

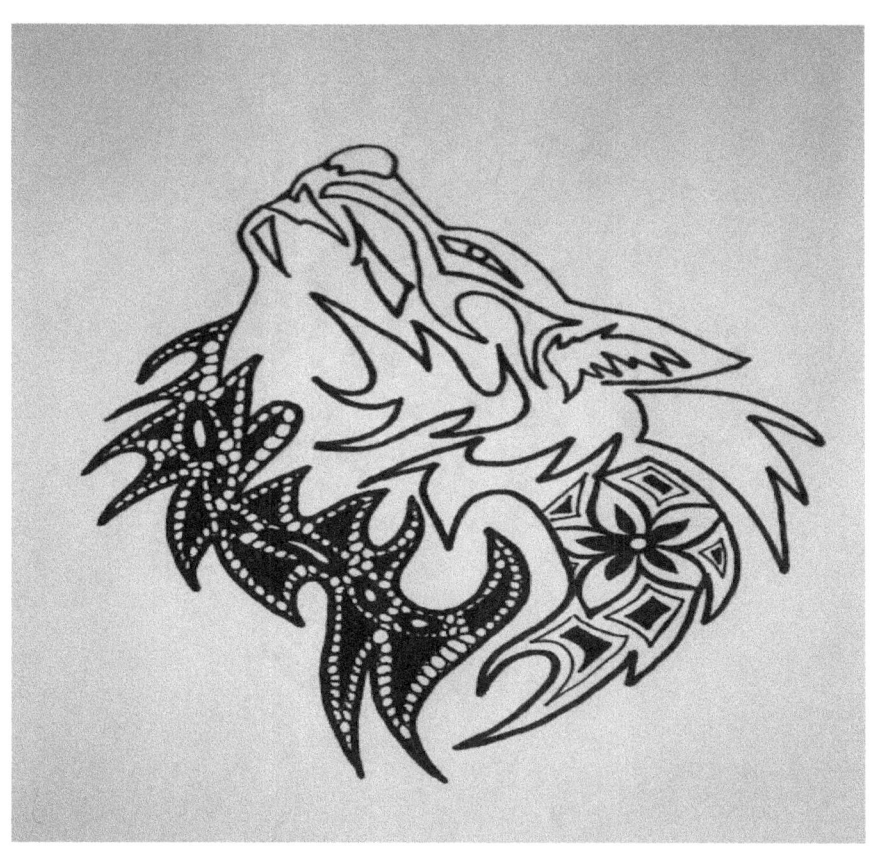

Step 4: Here you will complete the process of sketching out your lion's face, and to do that you will need to sketch out the whole mane like you see here.

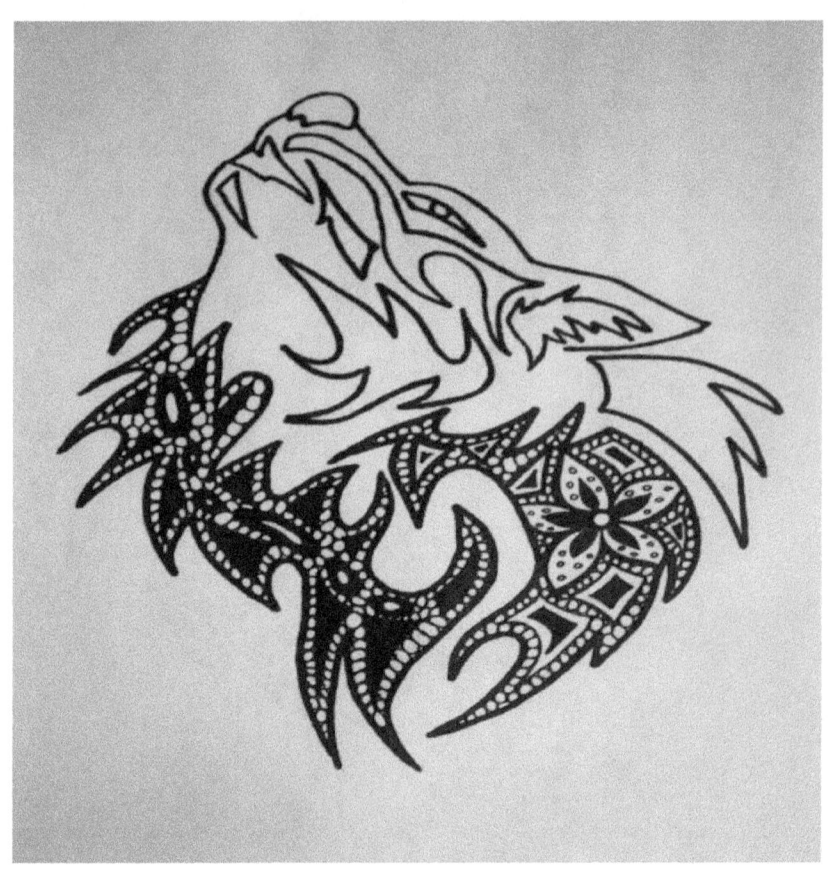

Step 5: Include some point of interest and definition by making the hair lines look like delicate streaming strands all through the lions mane.

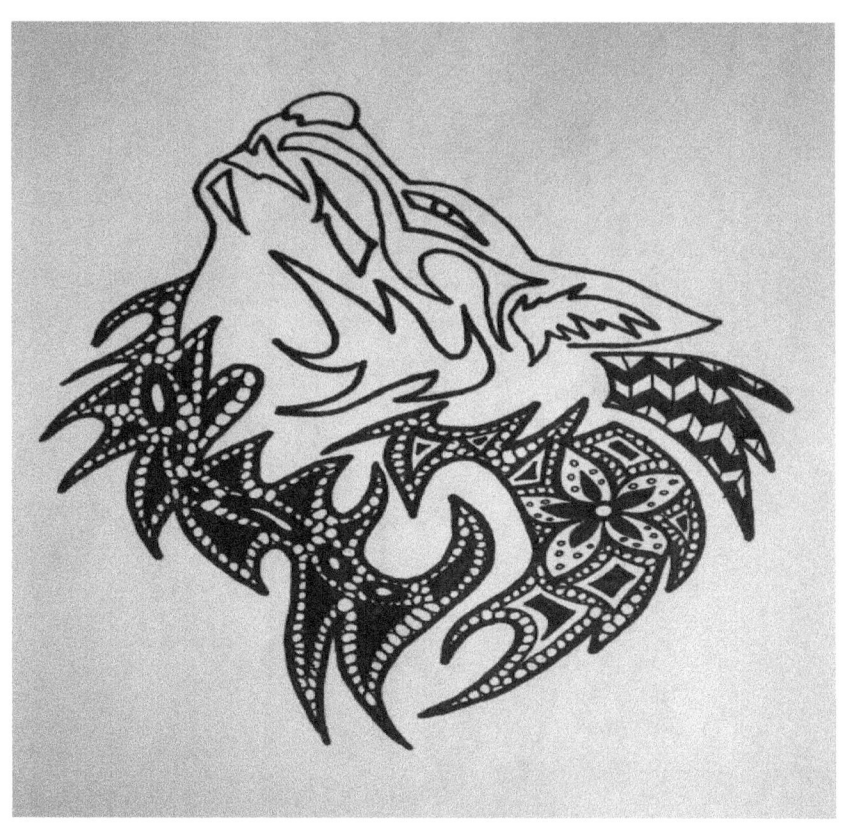

Step 6: Delete the rules and shapes that you attracted step one preceding you begin including so much detail and definition. Keep in mind the bristles peeps!

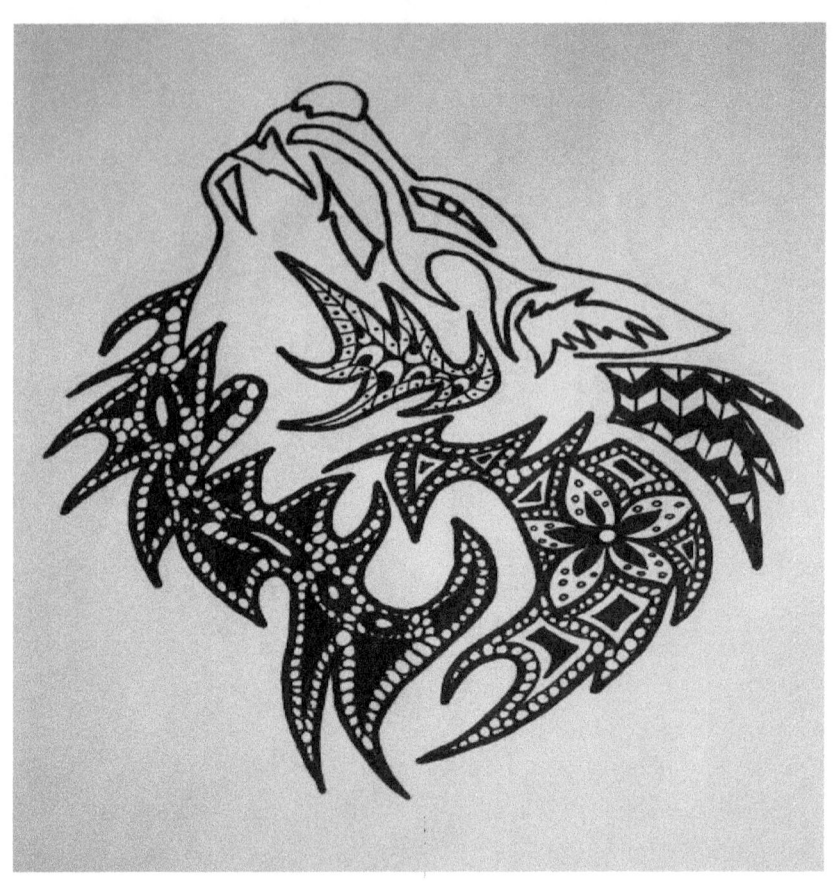

Step 7: Here is the means by which a completely drawn lion ought to look when finished. To draw a practical and straightforward mane, include tufts with each stroke.

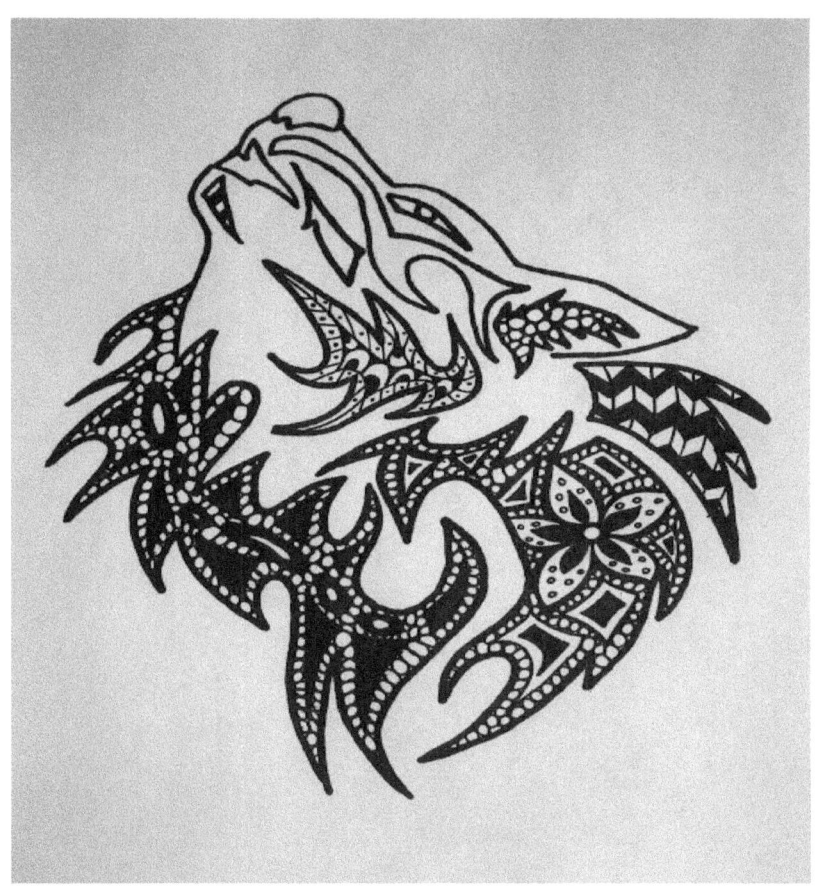

Step 8: From the front perspective of a lion, each of the four of their toes arc obvious and are curved up. What's more, when drawn in a 3/4 view, just three toes are noticeable.

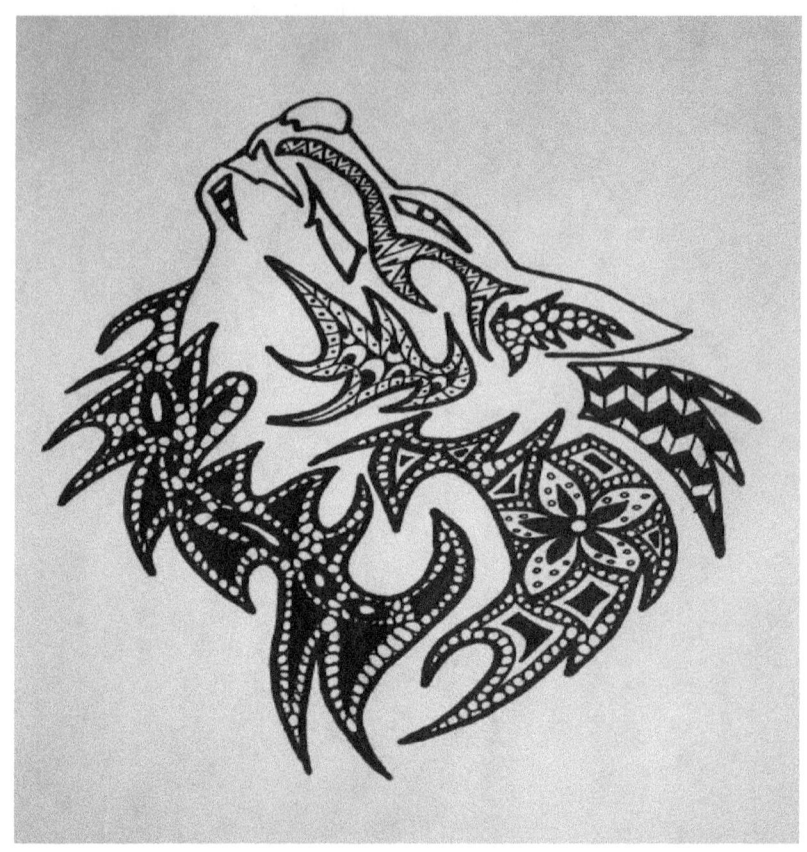

Step 9: This is the first drawing venture to drawing a lion. Start by drawing out one circle for the head, and after that draw out a major almond shape around the head for the lion's mane. Finally, include the facial rules.

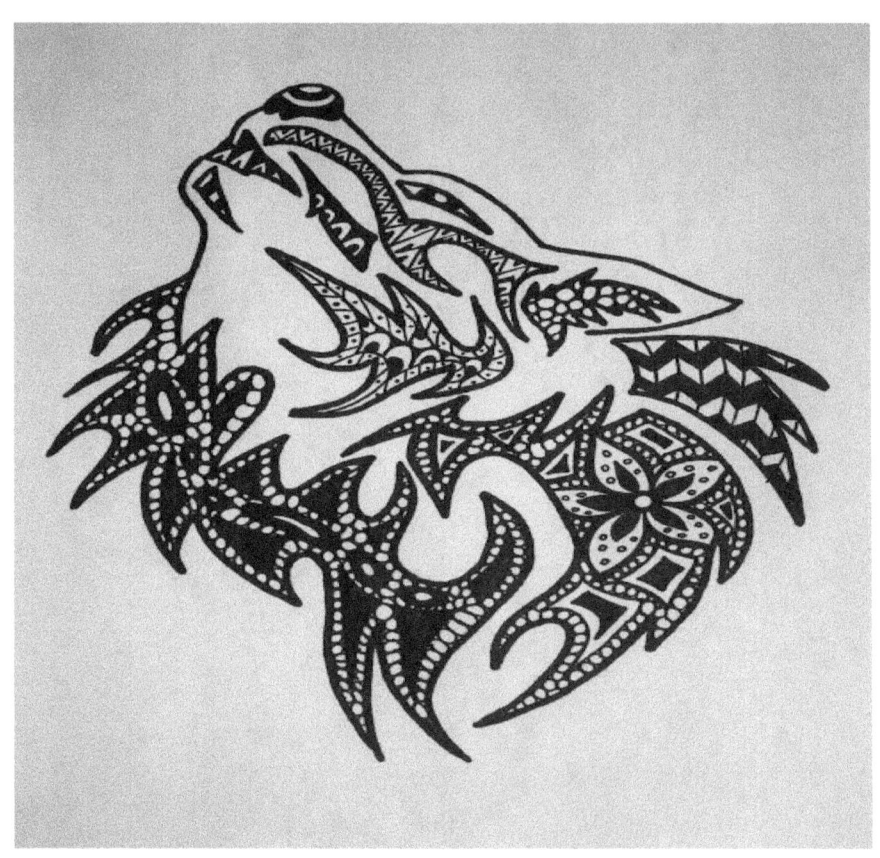

Step 10: Next, draw out the nose tip like you see here and ensure it is pleasant and wide. Keep in mind to draw in the line beginning from the base tip of the nose. This is the line that isolates the two cheeks or lips.

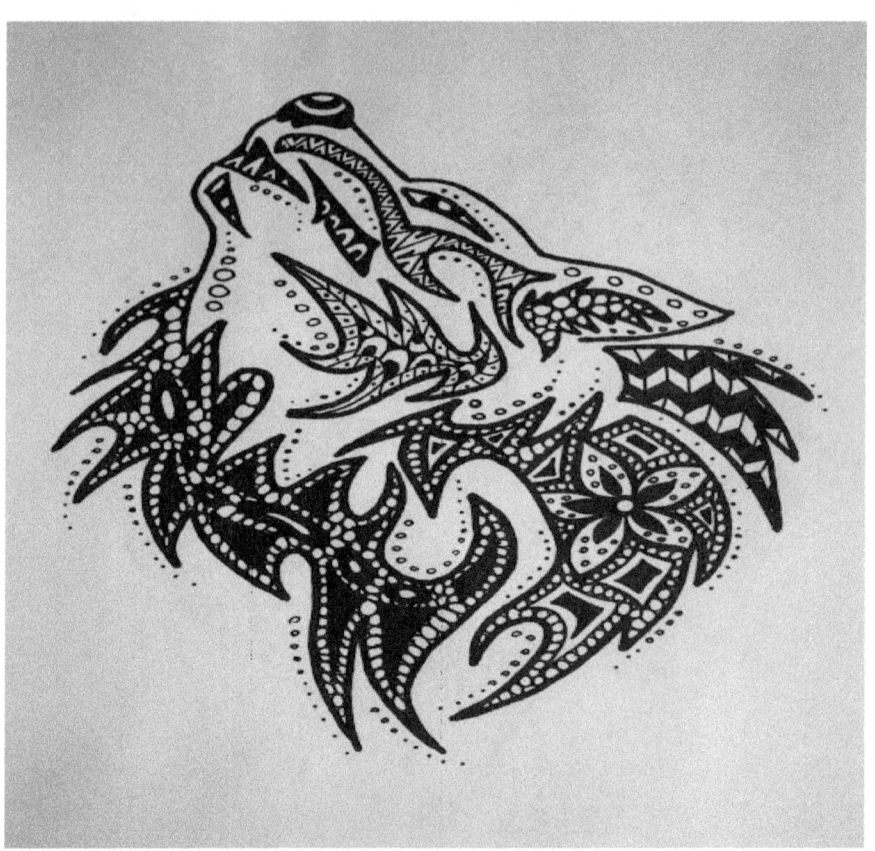

Step 11: This is the initial step to drawing the lion's body. Begin by drawing out the front legs and afterward the paws. As should be obvious the hooks are somewhat uncovered.

Step 12: Here is the thing that your brute looks like when you are all done. Presently you can simply ahead and shading it into your preferring. I had a fabulous time showing you folks how to draw a lion. Go along with me next time for all the more drawing fun.

Chapter 2 – How to draw a Zebra

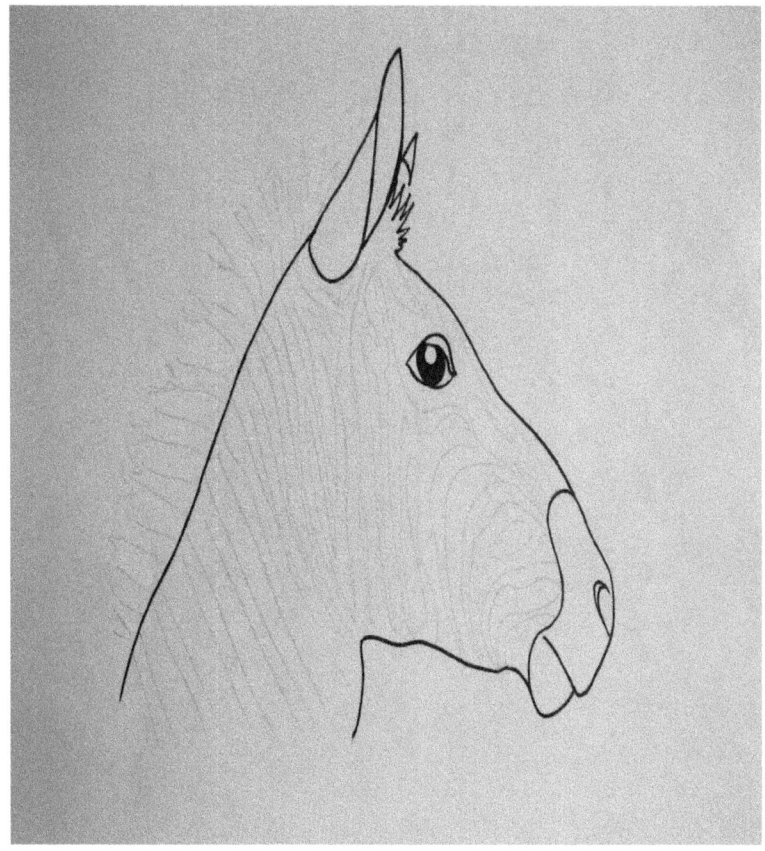

Step 1: Begin by picking your pencils. I utilized a HB pencil for sketching/shading, a 4B pencil for dim shading, and a 4H pencil for light lines and shading. Everyone continues asking me where I get my pencils. In the event that you go to finalprodigy.com and click on "workmanship supplies" in the menu you can discover the greater part of the supplies that I utilize.

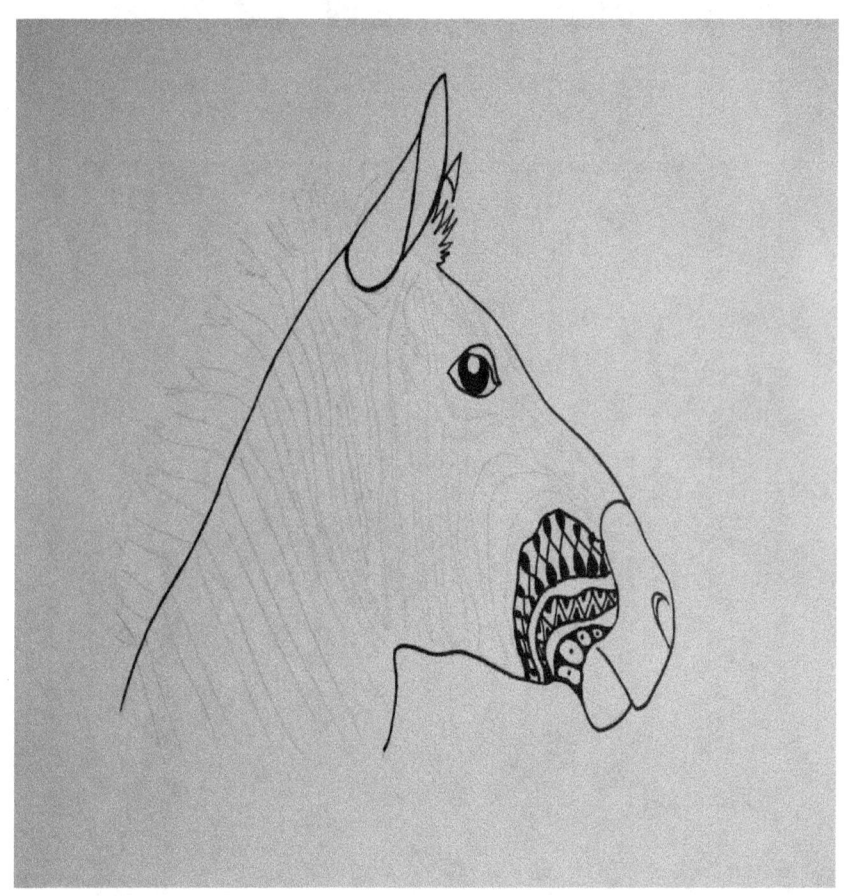

Step 2: Begin with a light sketch of the zebra head. Utilize the rules on the off chance that you require them.

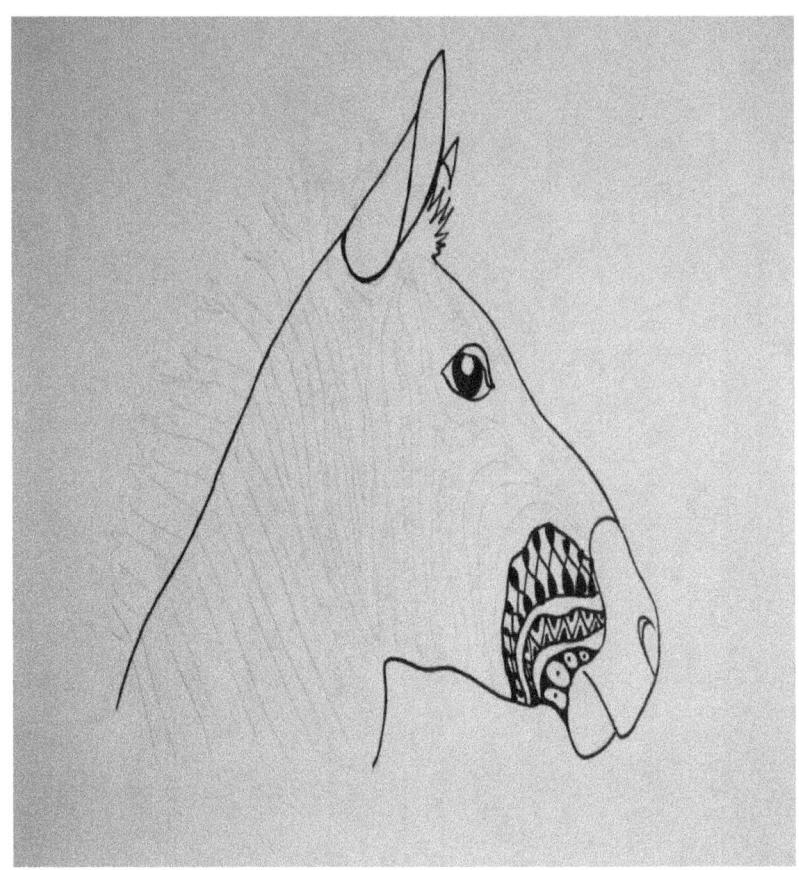

Step 3: Your sketch ought to wind up looking something like this. Attempt to eradicate any lines that you needn't bother with.

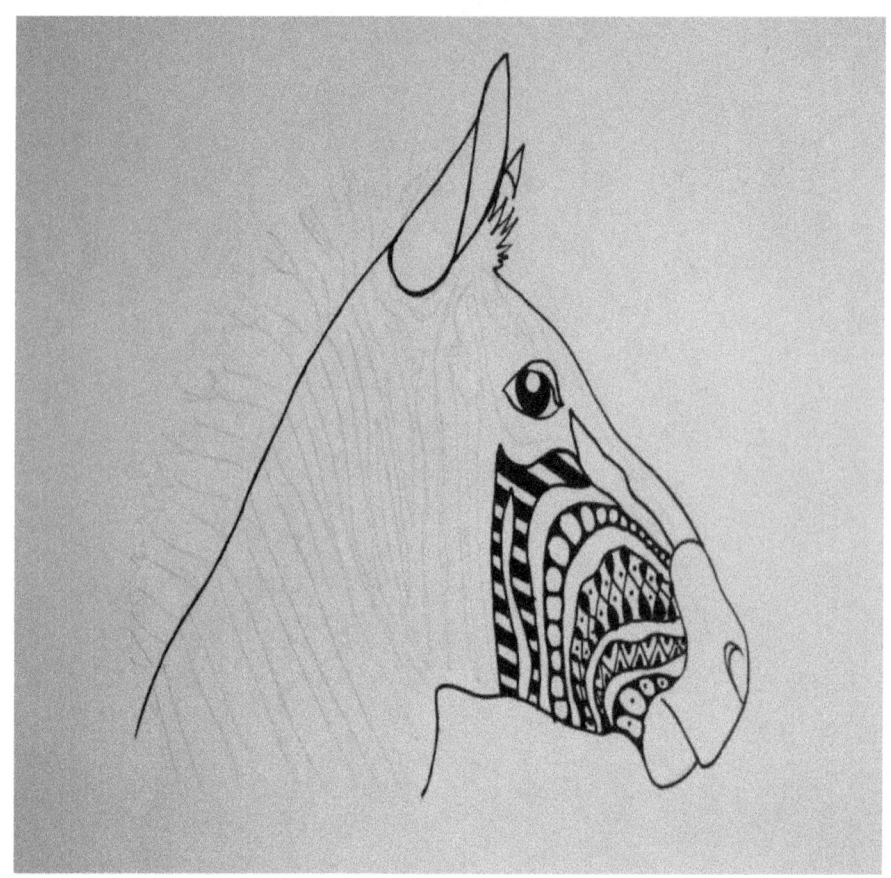

Step 4: Presently generally shade the nose and eyes. Try not to stress a lot over subtle elements at this moment. Shade in a couple stripes on the head and neck. These will go about as aides for whatever remains of the stripes.

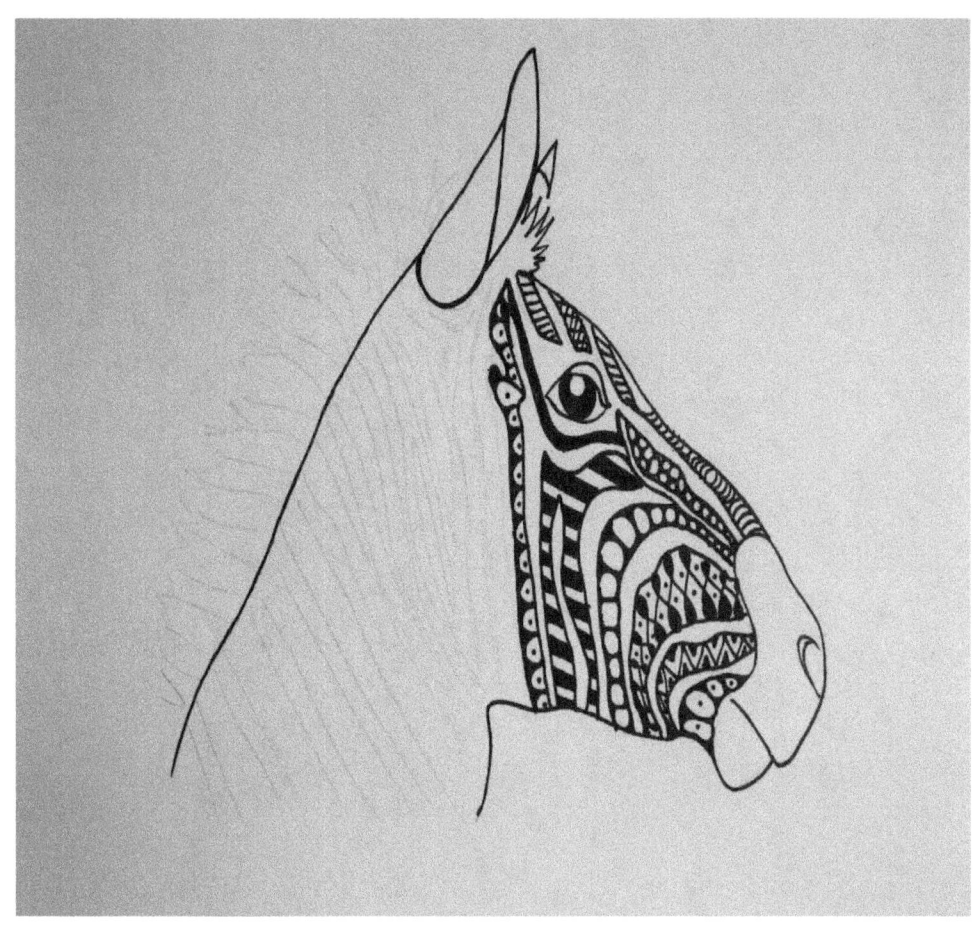

Step 5: While as yet utilizing a HB pencil, shade in the nose, characterize the ear and gently shade in the stripes on the head.

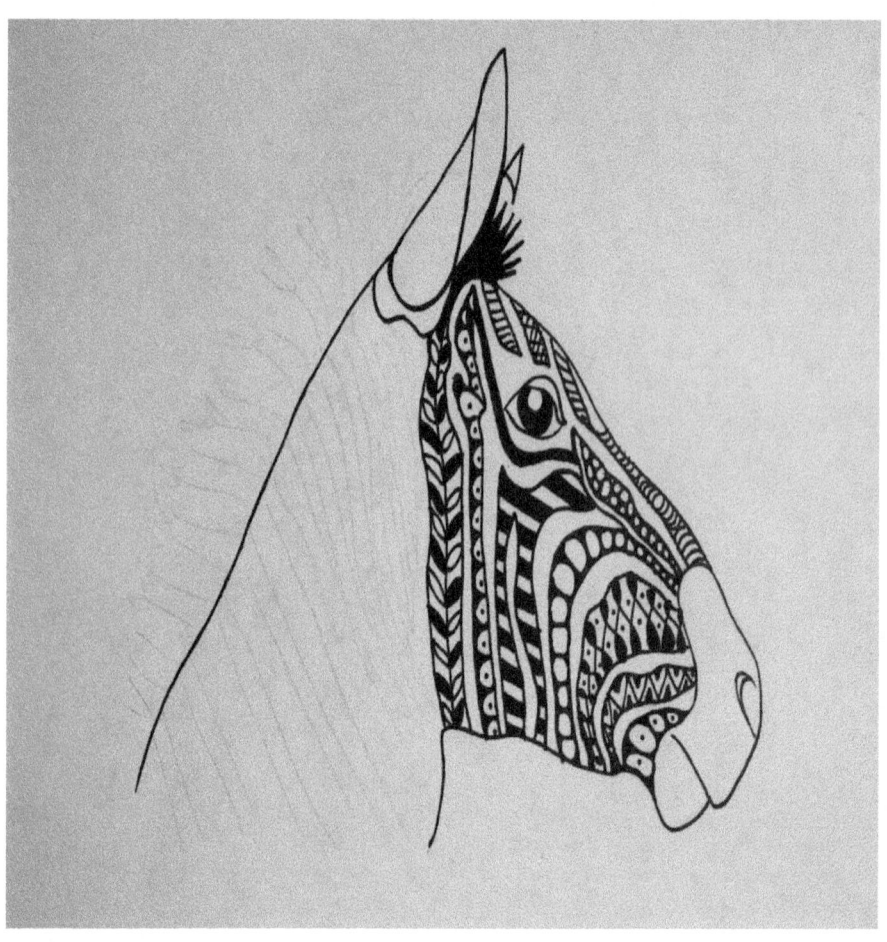

Step 6: Presently shade in the stripes on the neck and mane.

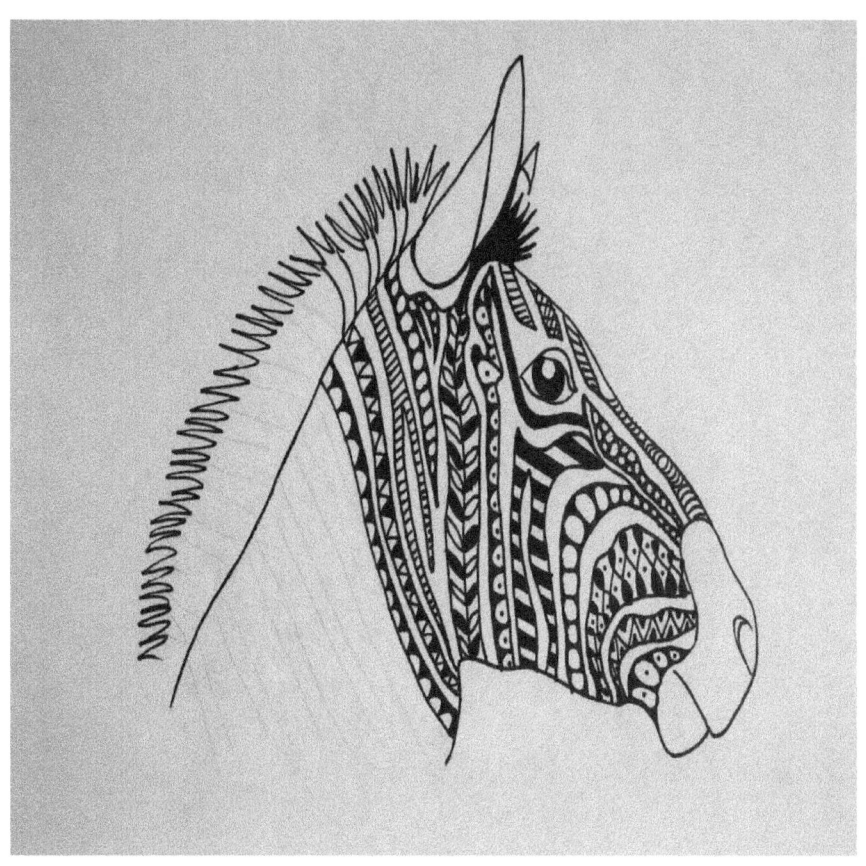

Step 7: Utilize a 4B pencil to gently shade out of sight. Try not to press down hard. Have a go at sketching as delicately as could be expected under the circumstances. After that utilization a mixing stump to mix in your experience.

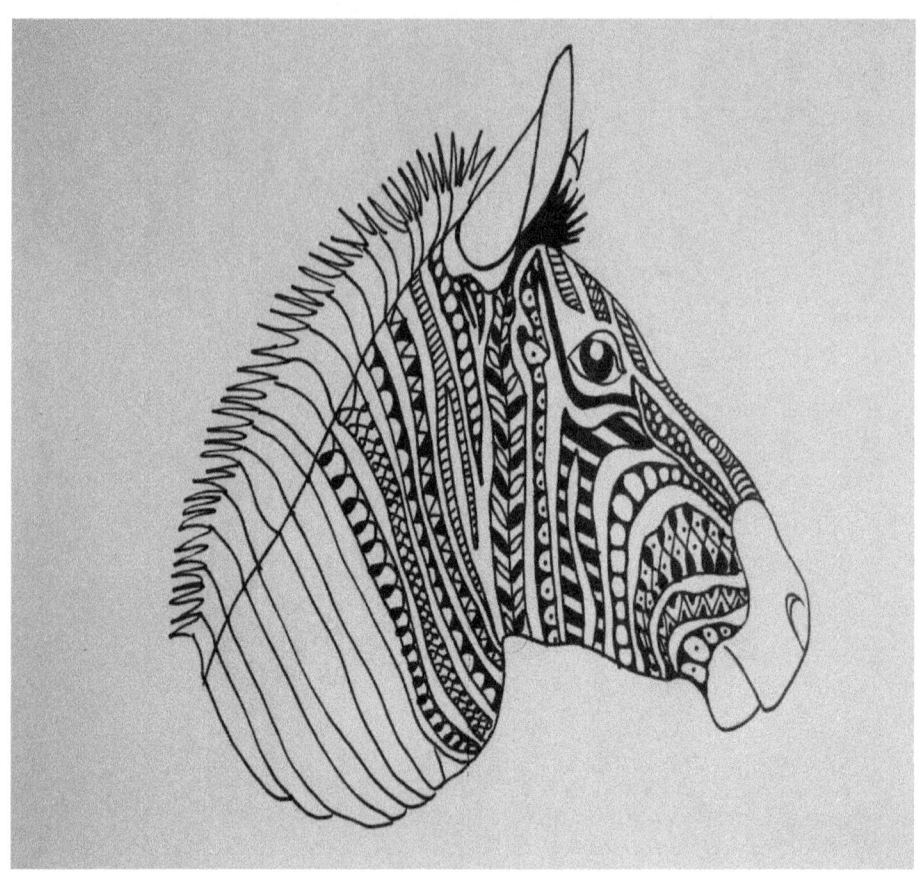

Step 8: Characterize the eyes and begin take a shot at the gag. The most effortless approach to make you're shading as dull as could be expected under the circumstances is to softly put down a layer of shading with a 4B pencil then run over that with a HB pencil. You can see the layer of 4B on the gag before utilizing a HB pencil.

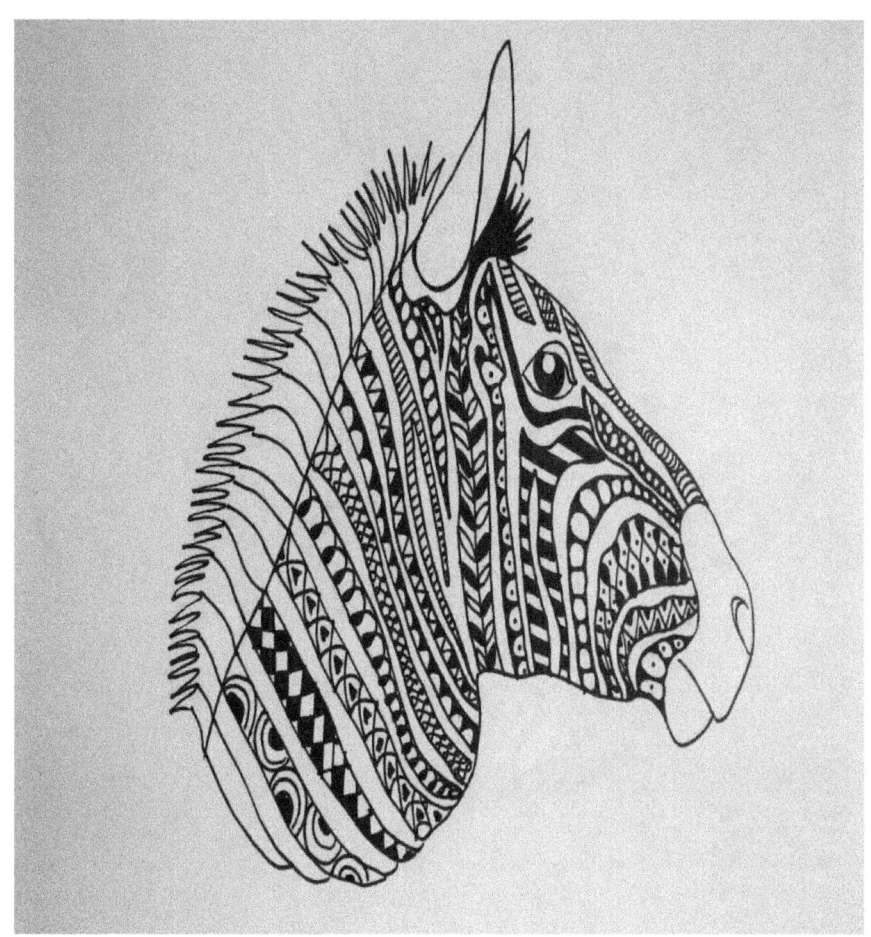

Step 9: Run over the gag with a HB pencil to obscure and smooth out your shading. Utilize a mixing stump sparingly. You would prefer not to smooth away the greater part of your surface. After that utilization the 4B to softly shade over the temple stripes.

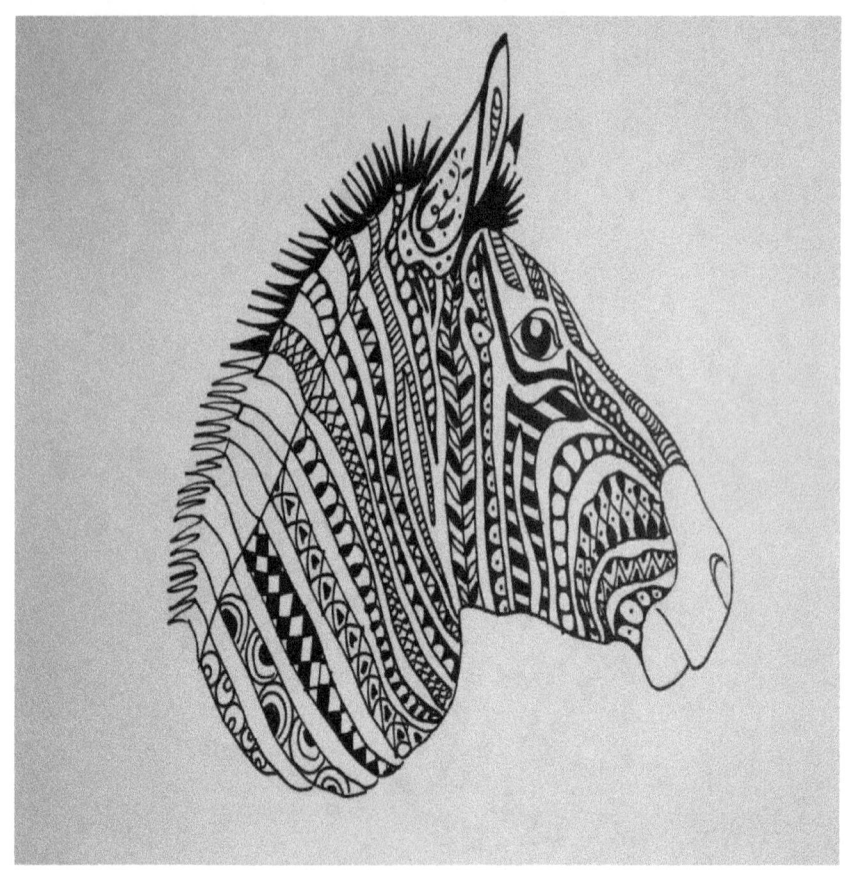

Step 10: Utilize a 4B pencil to shade over the stripes over whatever is left of the head and ears.

Step 11: Utilize a HB pencil to go over the stripes. Utilize a 3H pencil on the lighter ear hairs.

Step 12: Utilize a 4H pencil to obscure the focal point of the white stripes a bit. Leave the white around the edges. This will make the dark stripes pop out.

Step 13: Utilize a 4B pencil to shade over the neck stripes.

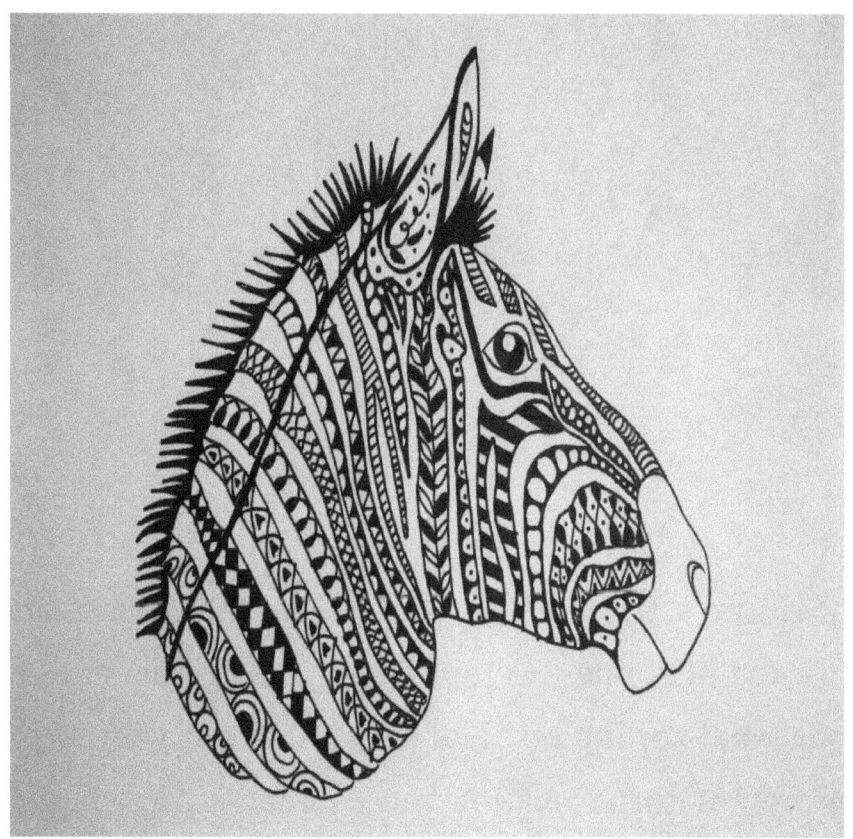

Step 14: Utilize a HB pencil to go over the dim stripes and a 4H pencil on the light ones.

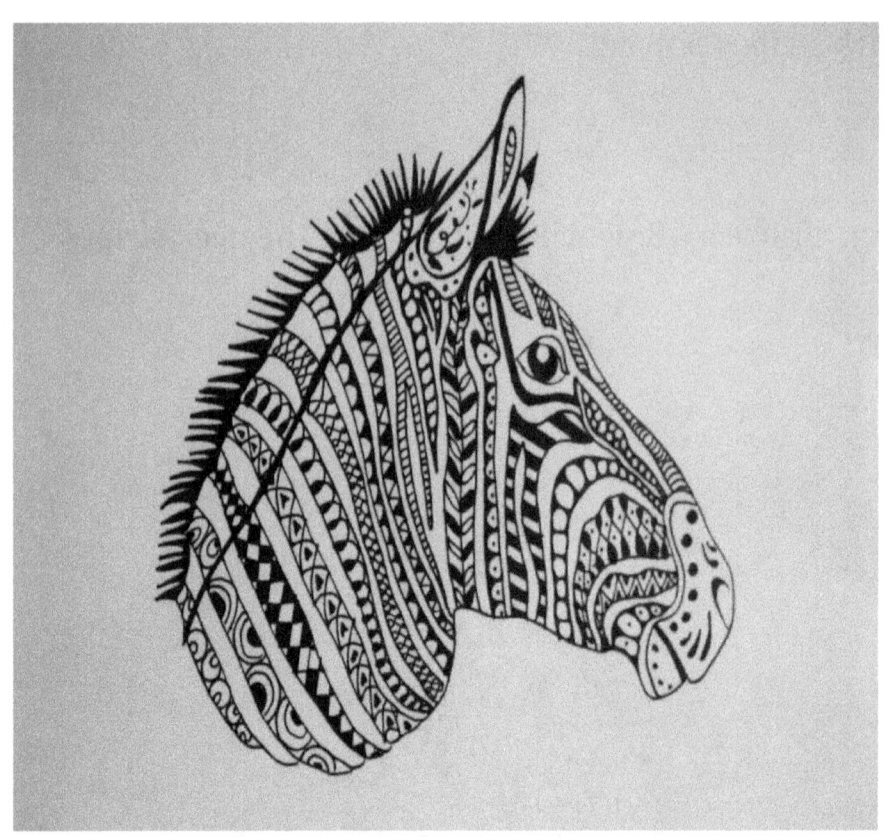

Step 15: Utilize a HB pencil to go over the dim stripes and a 4H pencil for the light ones. Completion up the going so as to draw over your points of interest and smoothing out your experience. Tell me how it turns out for you. Remarks and inquiries are welcome!

Chapter 3 – How to draw a tiger

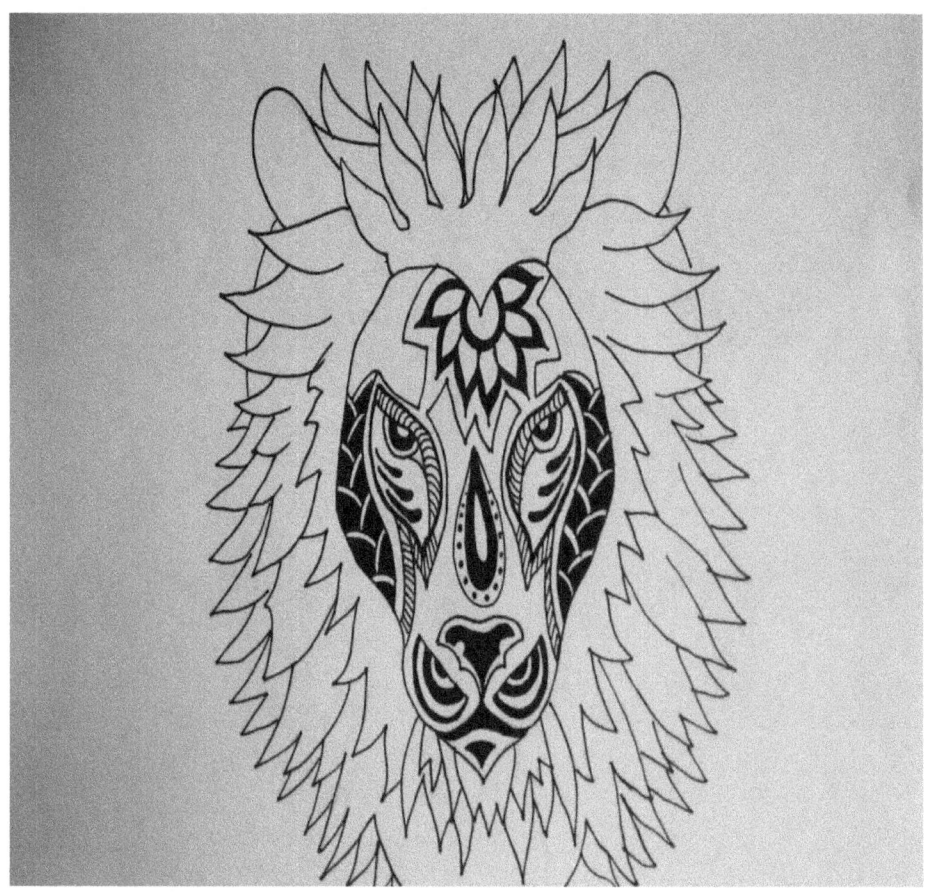

STEP 1. Before we begin I'll demonstrate to you which instruments I'm going to use in this instructional exercise. - Pencils of different hardness: HB, 2B, 4B and 8B. - Mechanical pencil with 0.5mm HB or 2B lead.

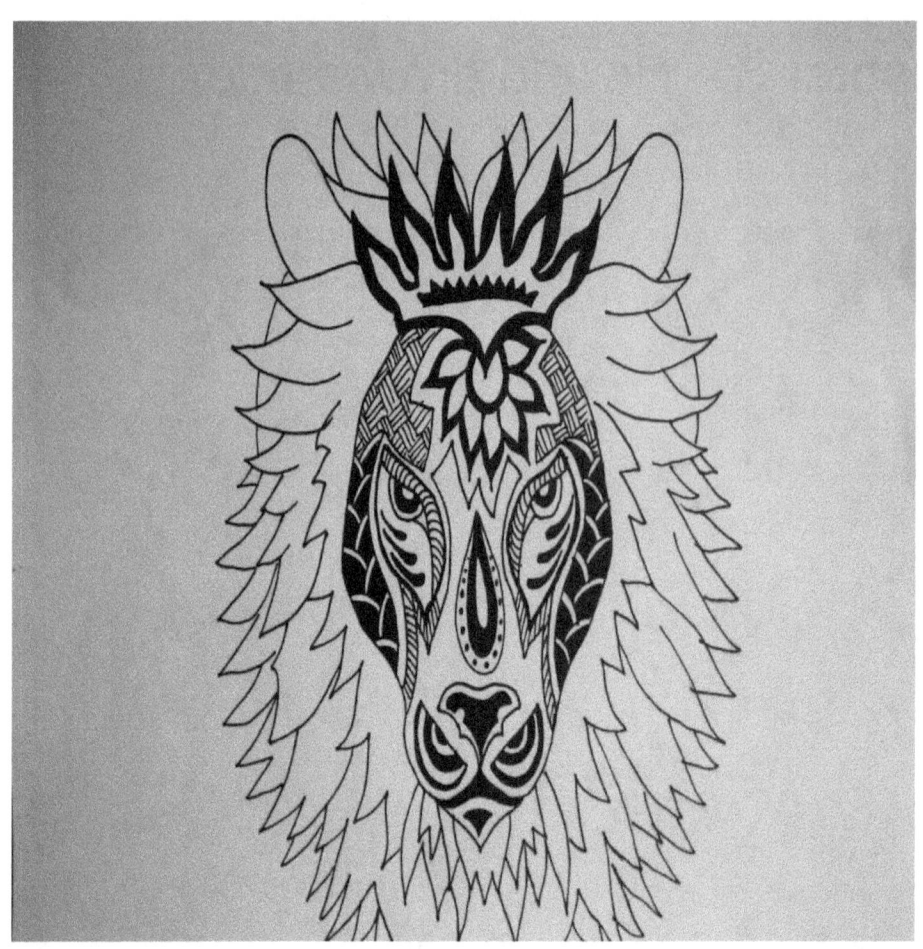

Step 2: On the off chance that you require it, draw the rules like you find in the picture. Attempt to keep the right extents of the diverse parts of the Tiger. At the point when the rules are done and you think they are right, begin the genuine drawing. What you are doing now will direct you in the following steps so include every one of the points of interest you believe are critical. For this stride I've utilized HB pencil.

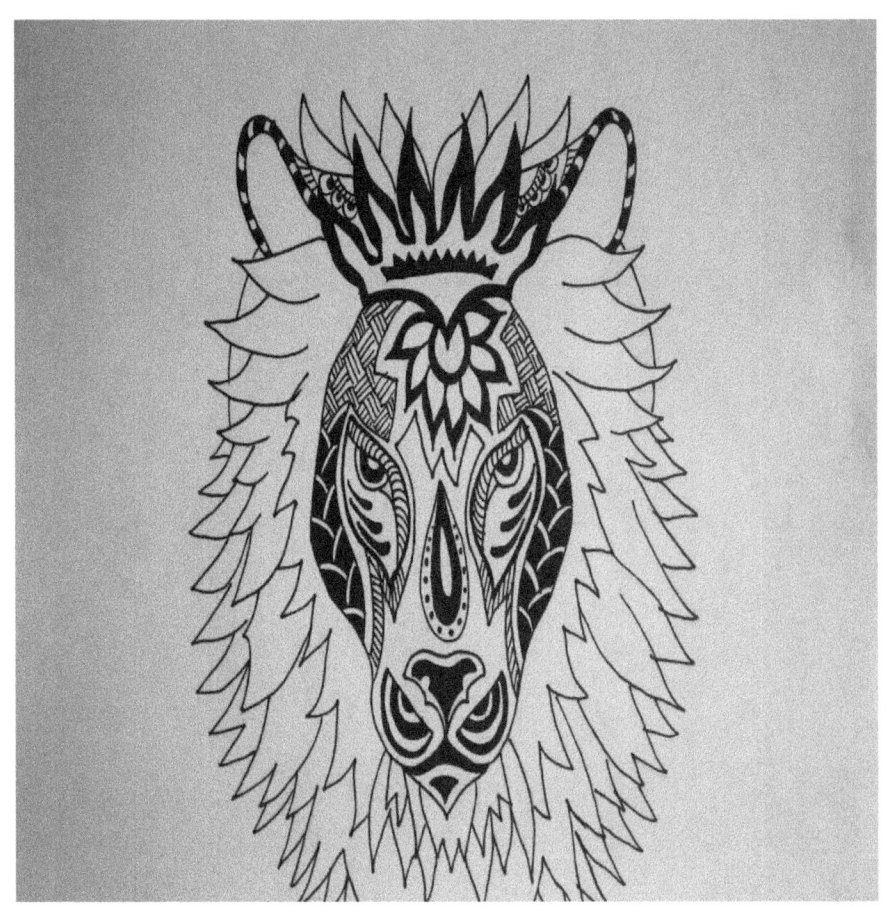

Step 3: Presently a few recommendations and traps to offer you on the off chance that you some assistance with having issues drawing the tiger. - When you draw the face look at the reference and streamline what you find in a progression of fundamental structures simple to duplicate.

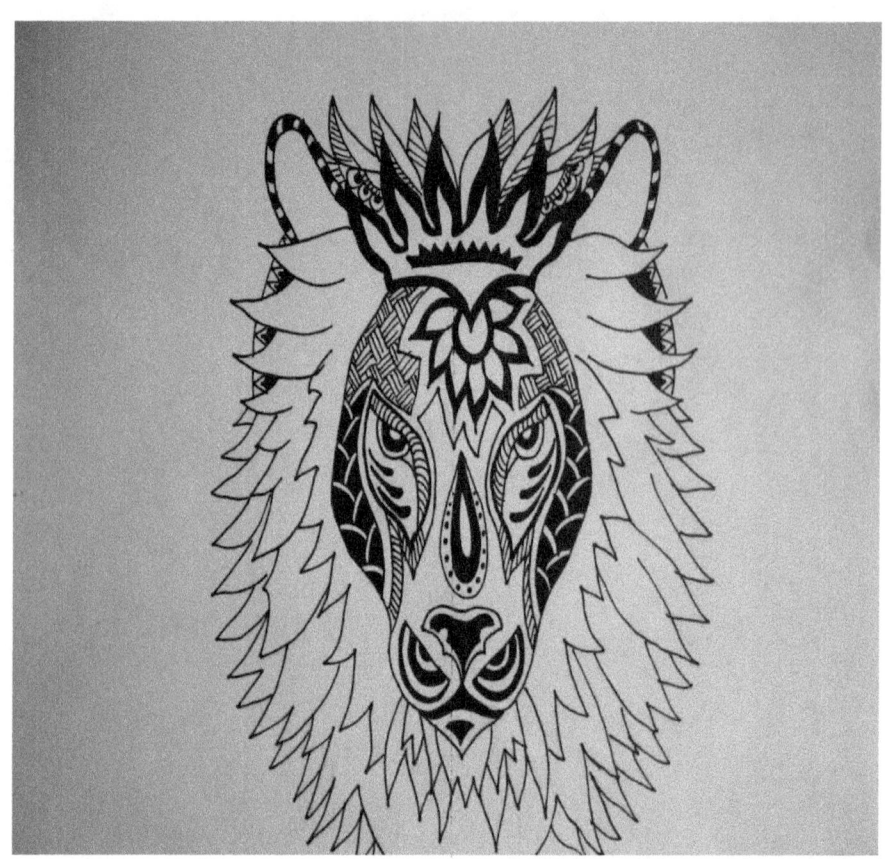

Step 4: Begin chipping away at the drawing from the darkest parts utilizing the 8B pencil. Change weight while drawing, press down the pencil just on the off chance that you need dark. Keep in mind to put a sheet of clean paper between your hand and the sheet on which you're working.

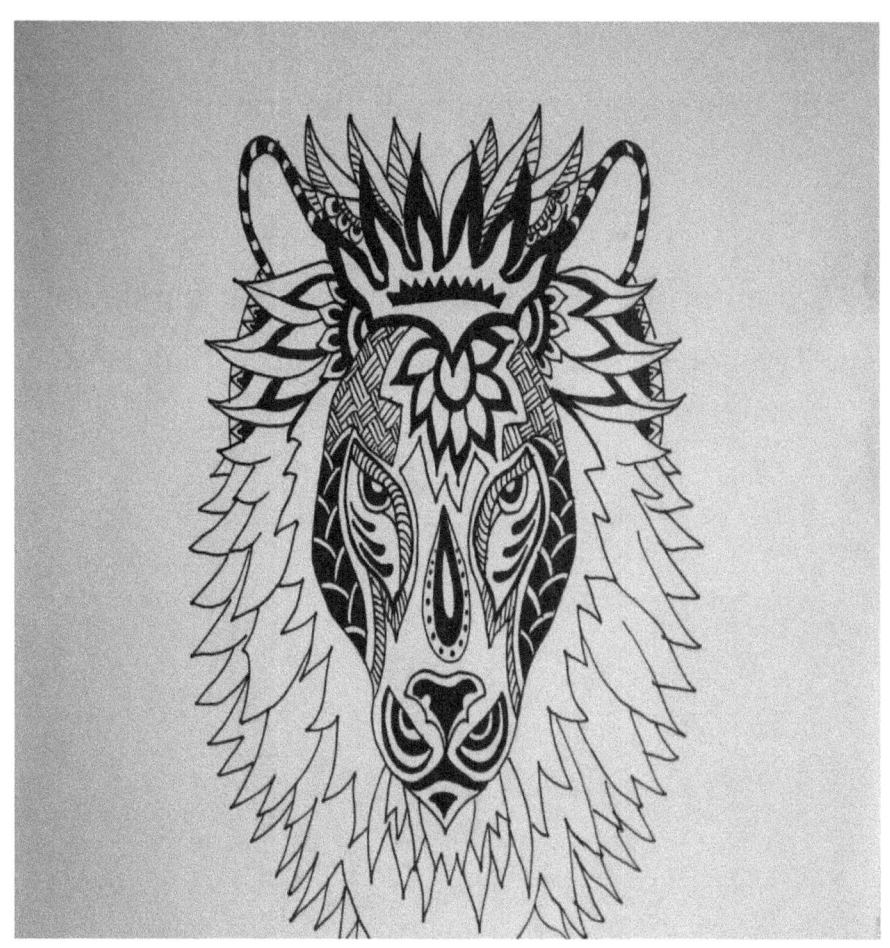

Step 5: At the point when the darkest parts has been settled, make a layer of base "shading" in the parts not touched by the light. Add more layers to make darker shadows. Despite everything i'm utilizing the 8B pencil.

Step 6: Do likewise on the head. Keep the paper clear where there are highlights and white hide.

Step 7: Utilize the paper stump to mix the graphite.

Step 8: Presently the shadows ought to look darker and more uniform. Try not to touch the ligther parts, thay need to stay clear.

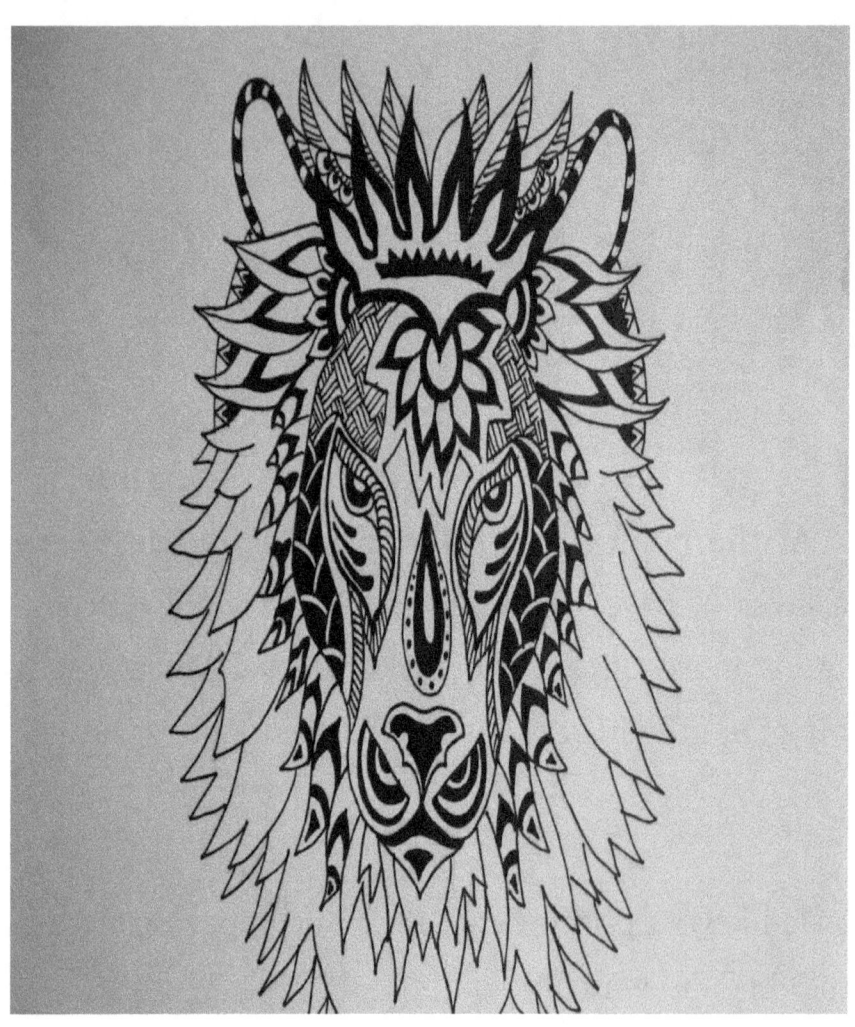

Step 9: The base of the drawing is done so we can add the stripes to the tiger. For this stride utilize the 8B pencil all around honed. The stripes are symmetric and distinctive for every person. Draw the round understudies and a tiny bit of shadow inside the eyes, then mix with the paper stump.

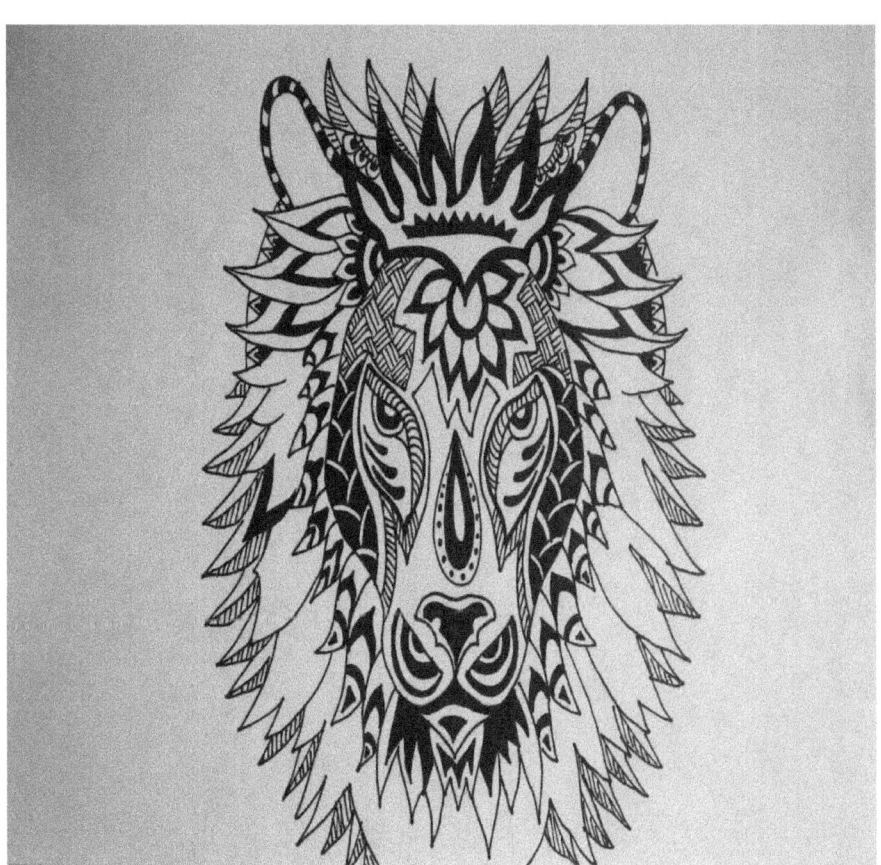

Step 10: Include two purposes of light inside the eyes with the eraser pencil or with a little bit of putty elastic. Keep drawing the stripes on the body of the tiger.

Step 11: When you're finished with the stripes this is the manner by which your tiger ought to look.

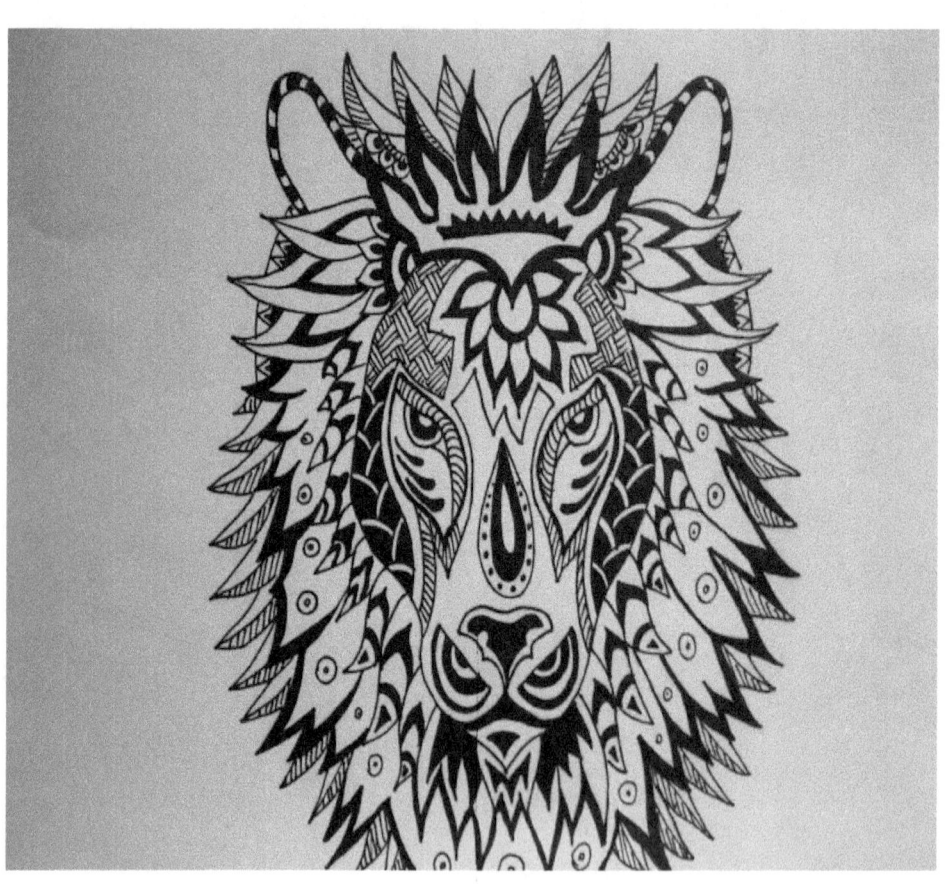

Step 12: We should complete with a "synopsis" of the primary different parts, from dark to white. The dark bolts show the dark parts, the darker ones. The blue bolts demonstrate the darker parts of the shadows, where they are close to the light. The red bolts demonstrate the edified parts. The yellow bolts show the purposes of highlights, where the paper is left white. I trust you loved this instructional exercise!

Step 13: Simply include a few shadows the stones and you're finished.

Chapter 4 – How to draw a Cheetah

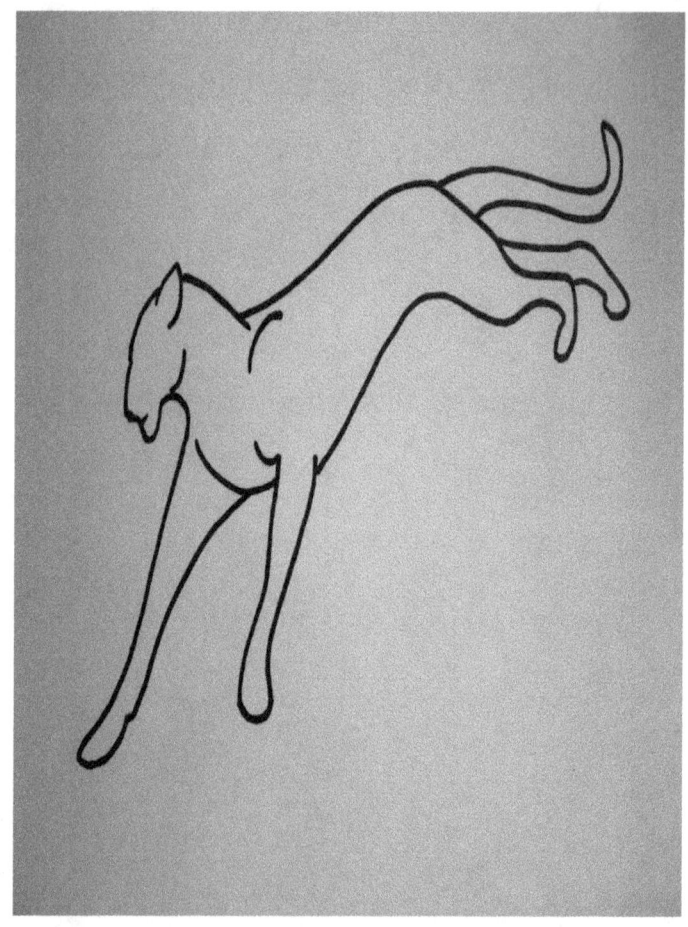

Step 1: We should begin the full body drawing the rules. Attempt to draw these aides precisely, as your future advances will rely on upon them. These rules assume as a part of an establishment. You don't need to draw the lines flawlessly thick, only comparative in sizes.

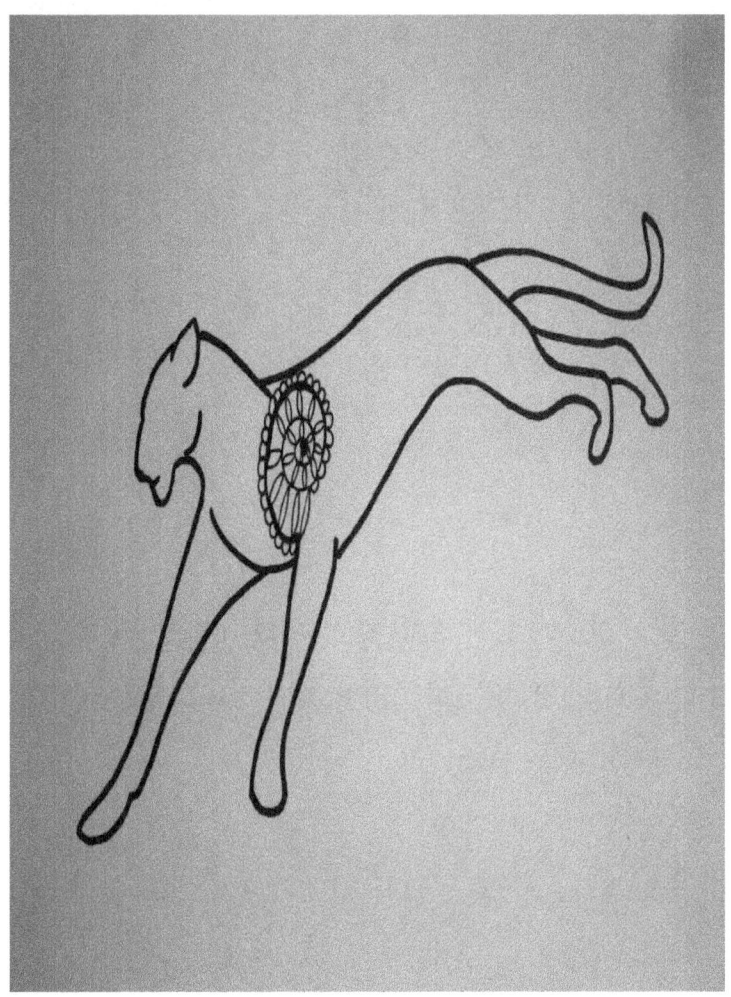

Step 2: Draw the head and the neck. The hide on the neck is somewhat more. Bear in mind to include the smaller than normal "protuberance" which closes at the shoulder region. This is the place the cheetah's projecting upper shoulder is unmistakable.

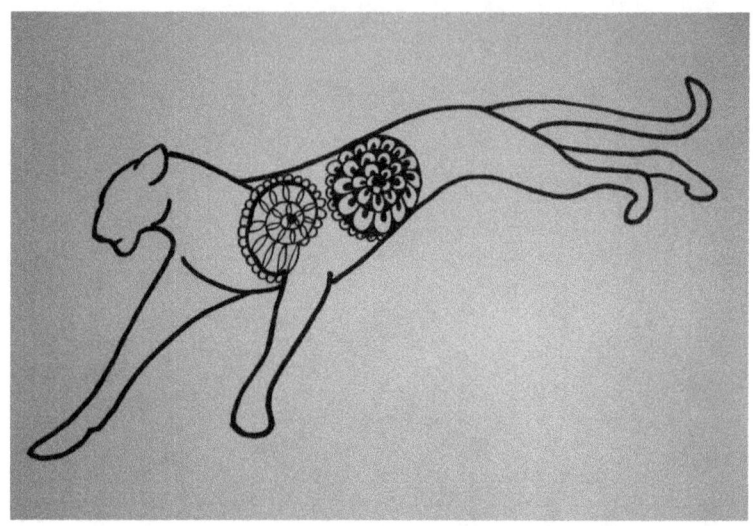

Step 3: Draw the shoulders and the long forelegs. The forelegs are long in light of the fact that cheetahs should be quick to chase down their fast moving prey.

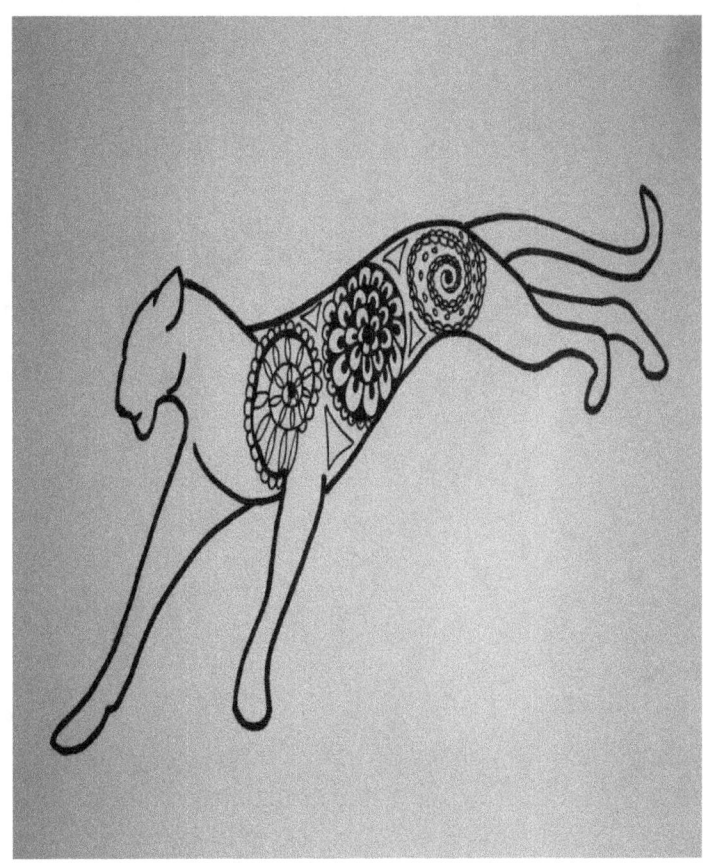

Step 4: Keep drawing the body utilizing the rules. Cheetahs' body is long and adaptable. Draw the rear legs and the long tail. Notice how the rear legs are longer contrasted with the forelegs. This is the place the cheetah's "energy" starts, the back legs. Have you've ever viewed a cheetah pursue it's dinner? The back legs almost achieve the length of the neck/mid-section.

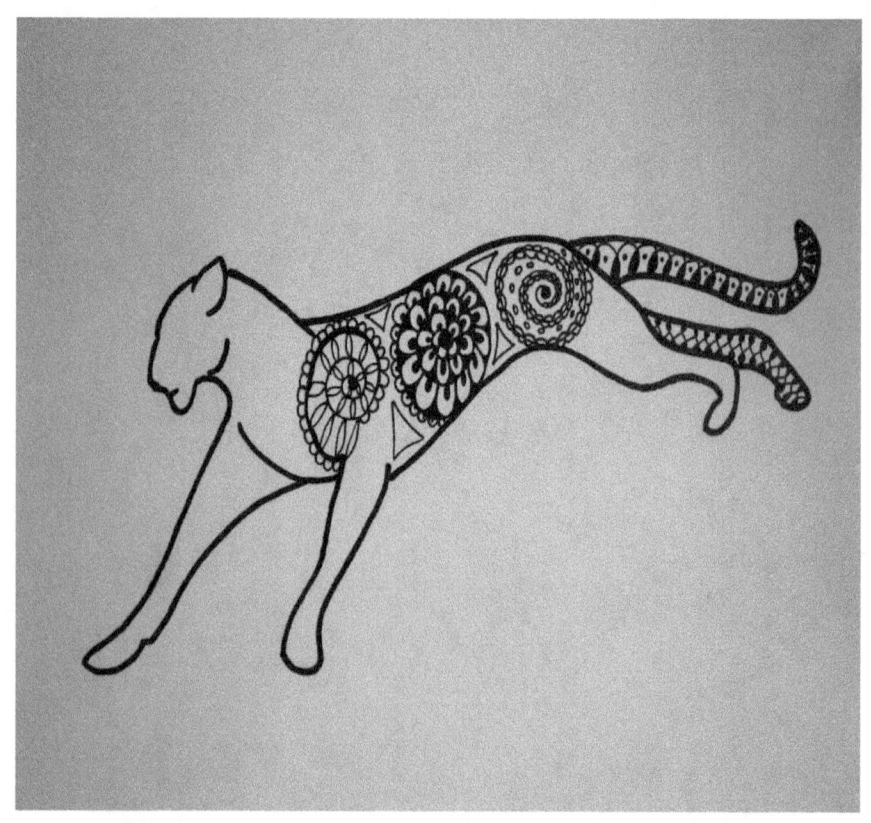

Step 5: Include nose, mouth, eyes and detail into the ears.

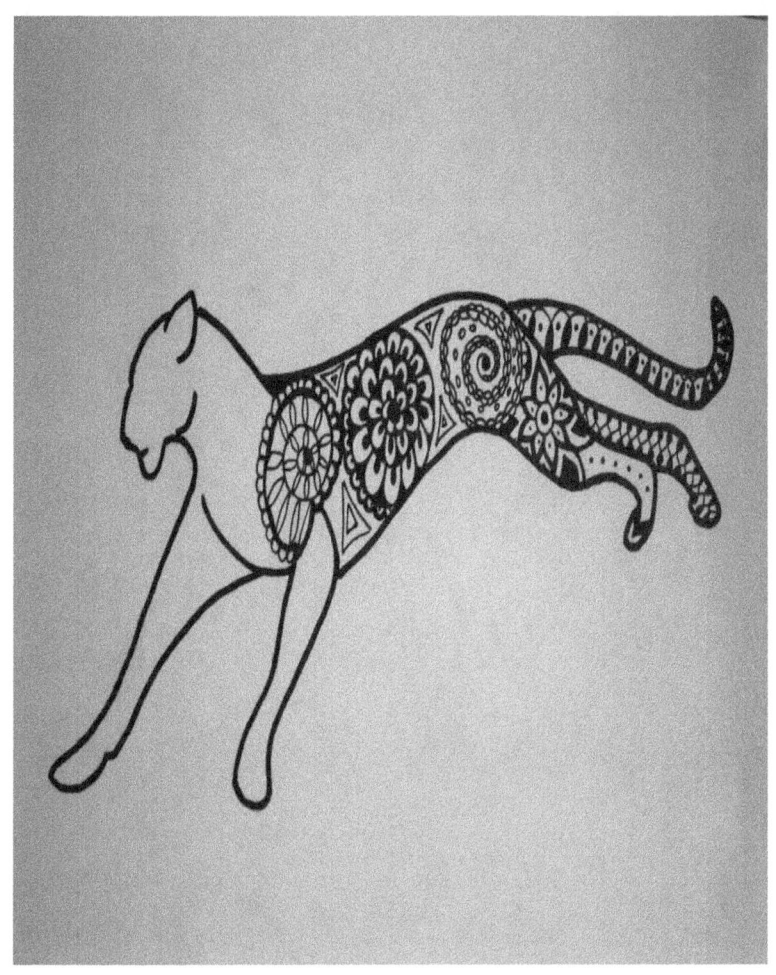

Step 6: Include the last subtle elements: stubbles, hide, hooks (cheetahs have no retractable paws) and a few lines that recommend the muscles. The cheetah is finished!

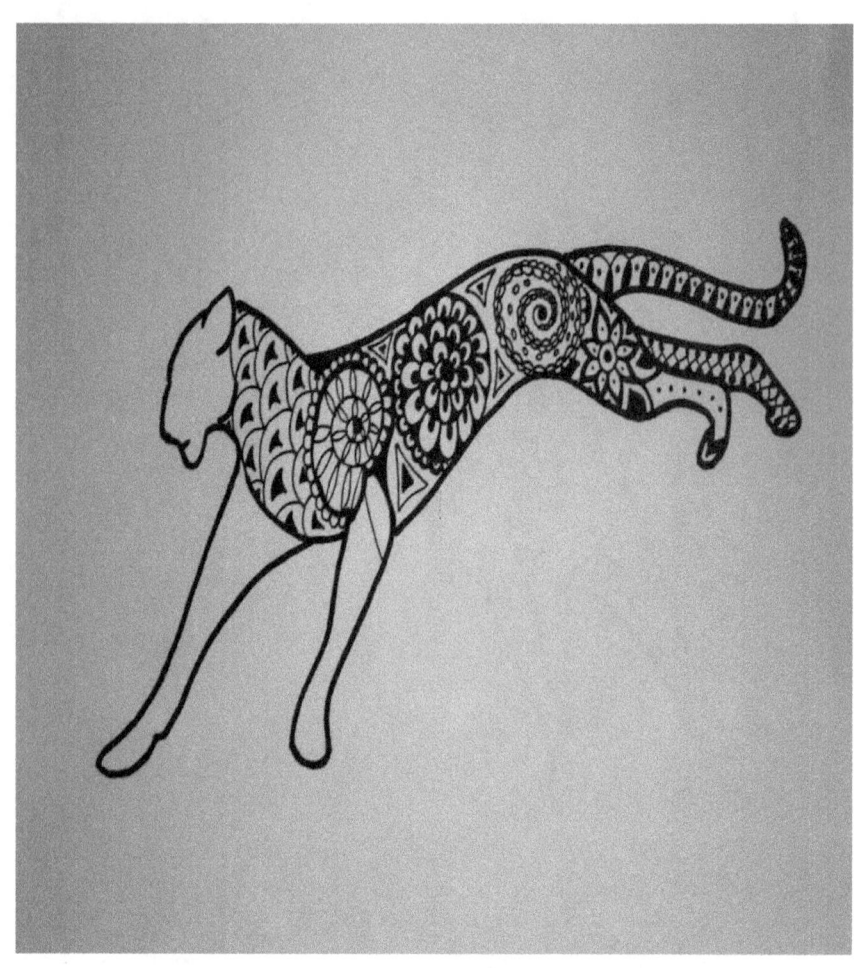

Step 7: Cheetahs' mantle is described by roundabout spots of different size. The spots are littler on the head and greater on the body. There are additionally dark markings on the face and on the ears. The tip of the tail is described by some dark rings that progressively transform into roundabout spots.

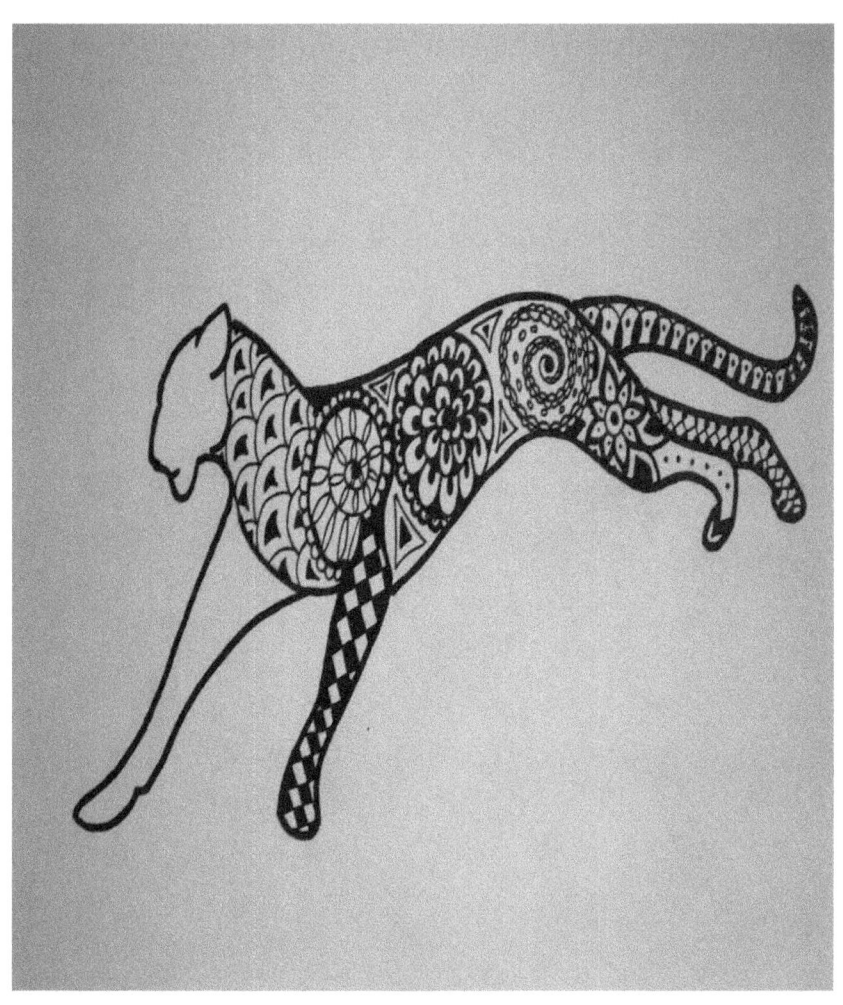

Step 8: Cheetahs paws are fundamentally the same to mutts' paws, truth be told they have no retractable hooks like alternate cats. In the first place, begin drawing the rules: straightforward lines and a circle for the wrist and one for the paw. Next, draw the leg and the paw. From the side perspective or semi 3/4 view, you can see three digits of the paw.

Step 9: Draw the rules of the running cheetah.

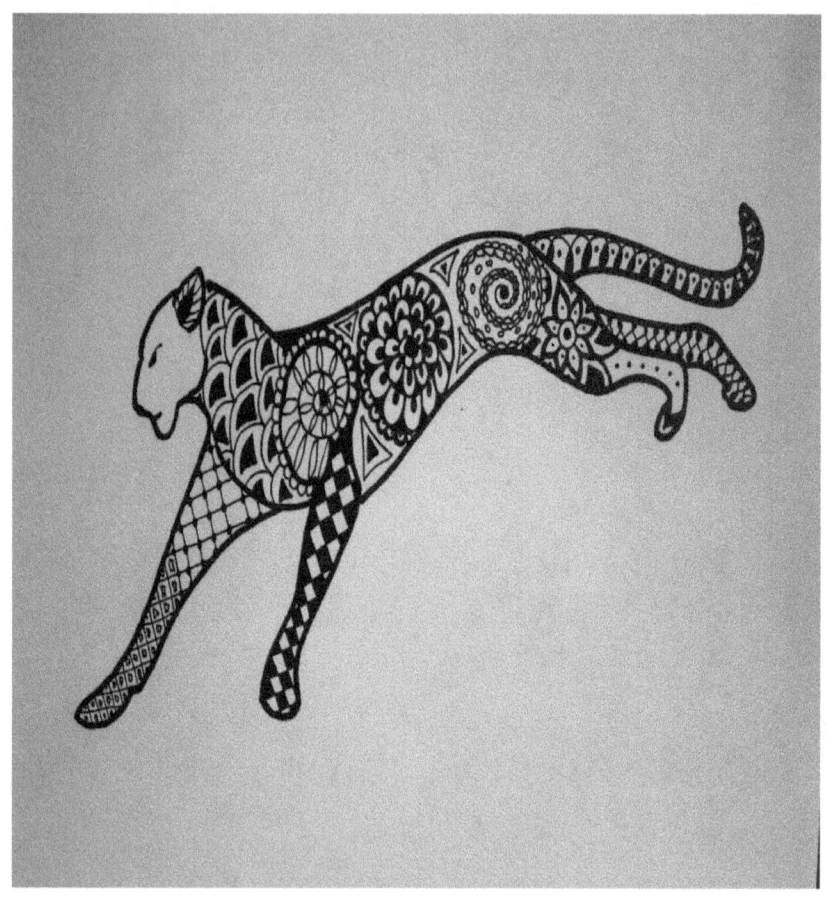

Step 10: Include the base type of the ears, two circles for the eyes and a triangle for the nose.

Step 11: Since the rules are done, we can begin drawing the lineart of head and neck.

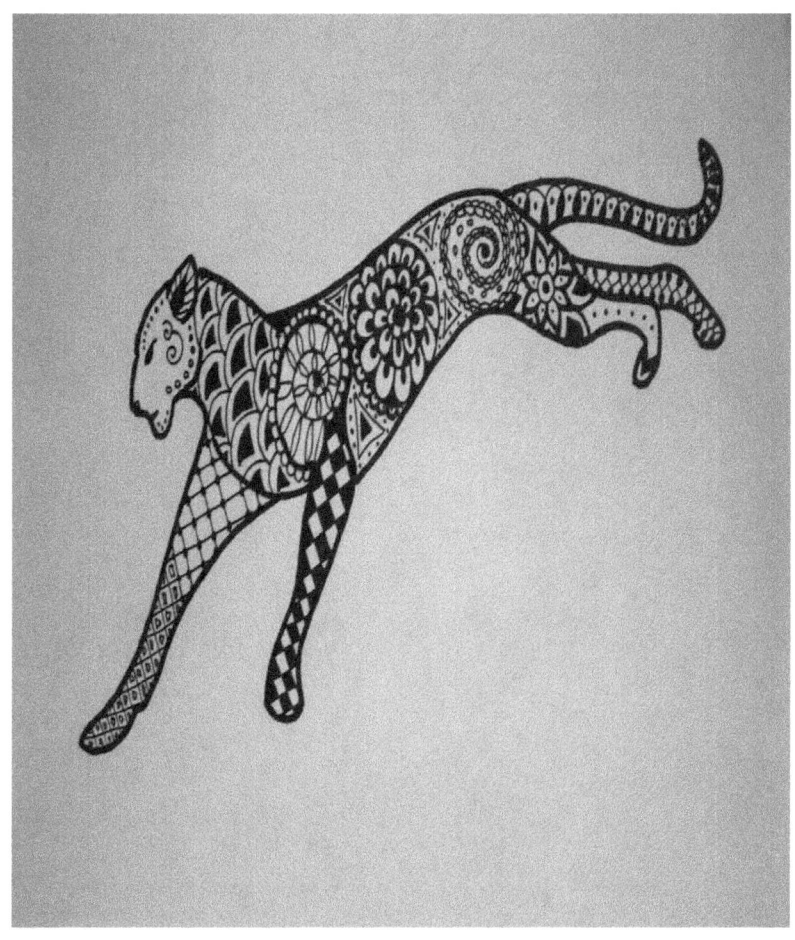

Step 12: Include a few points of interest the head: the marginally open mouth and the hide into the ears. At that point, include shoulders and forelegs.

Step 13: Include spots and bristles and you're finished!

Chapter 5 – How to draw a reindeer

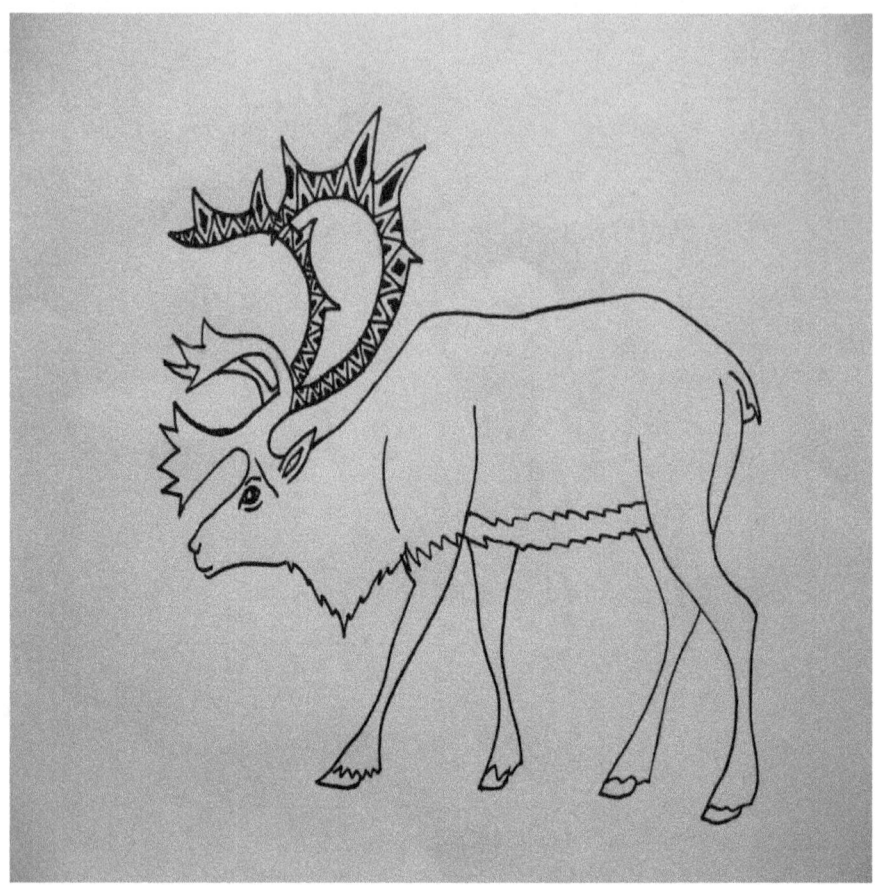

Step 1: How about we draw a reindeer might we? Begin by drawing the reindeer's head shape and include the facial rules, and in addition the rules for the horns and ears.

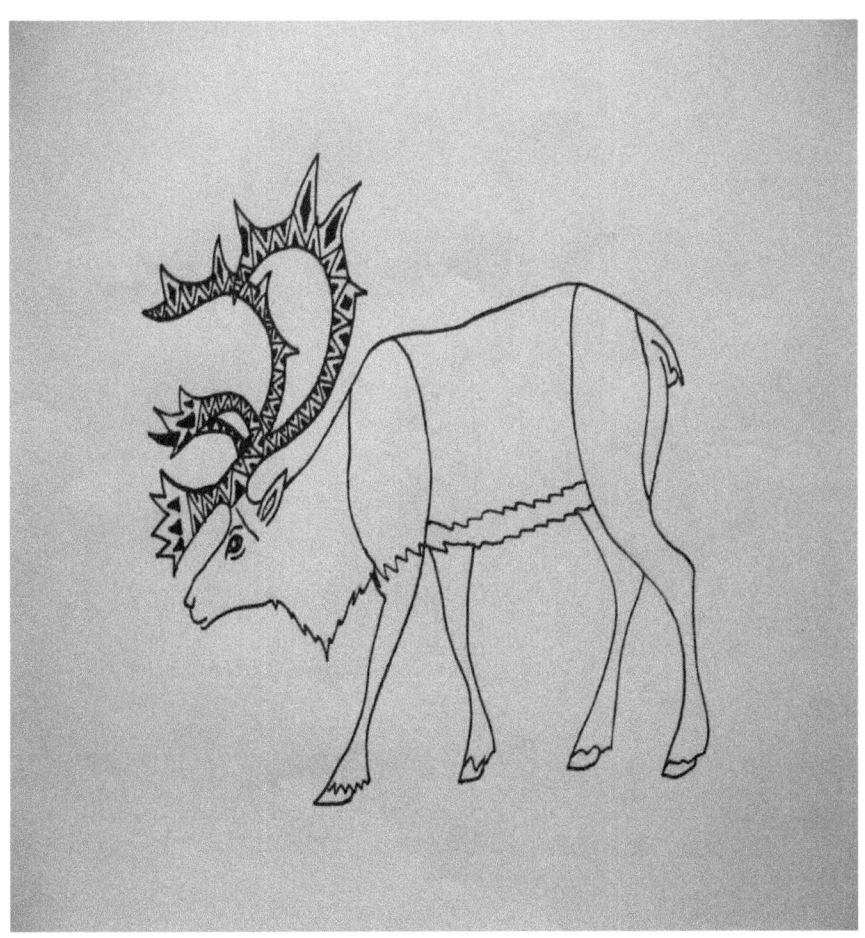

Step 2: Draw the shapes for the body and after that join the head shape to the reindeer's body with a neck line, and afterward draw the leg lines.

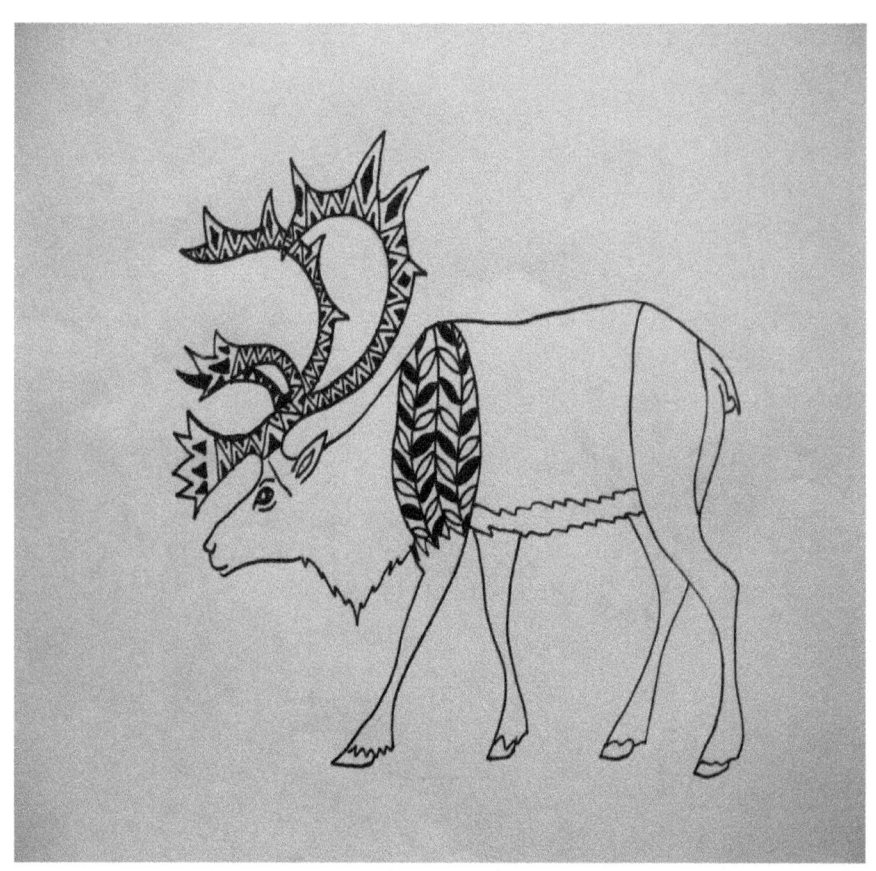

Step 3: You will now begin sketching out the state of the reindeer's head, face, cheeks, and after that draw out the tusks and ears totally. Drawing reindeer prongs is really simple.

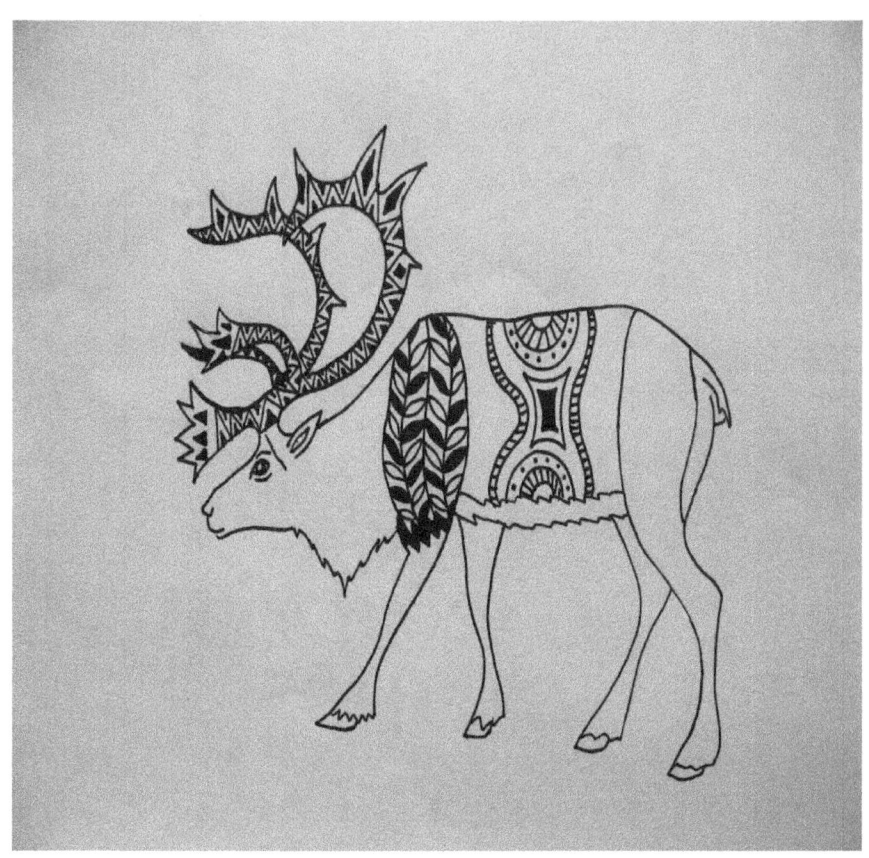

Step 4: Next sketch in some hair on the highest point of the head, and also in the middle of the eyes as well as eyebrows. Presently draw the nose and extension, and afterward sketch out the state of the mid-section.

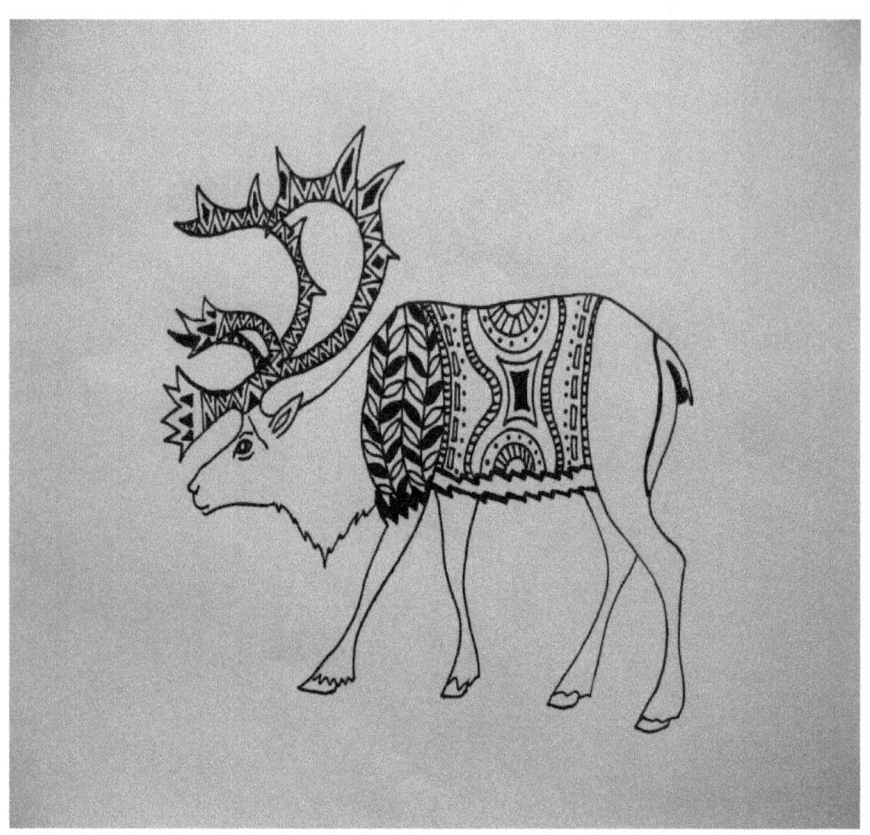

Step 5: Utilizing the facial rules you will draw the state of the reindeer eyes,m and after that draw the mouth.

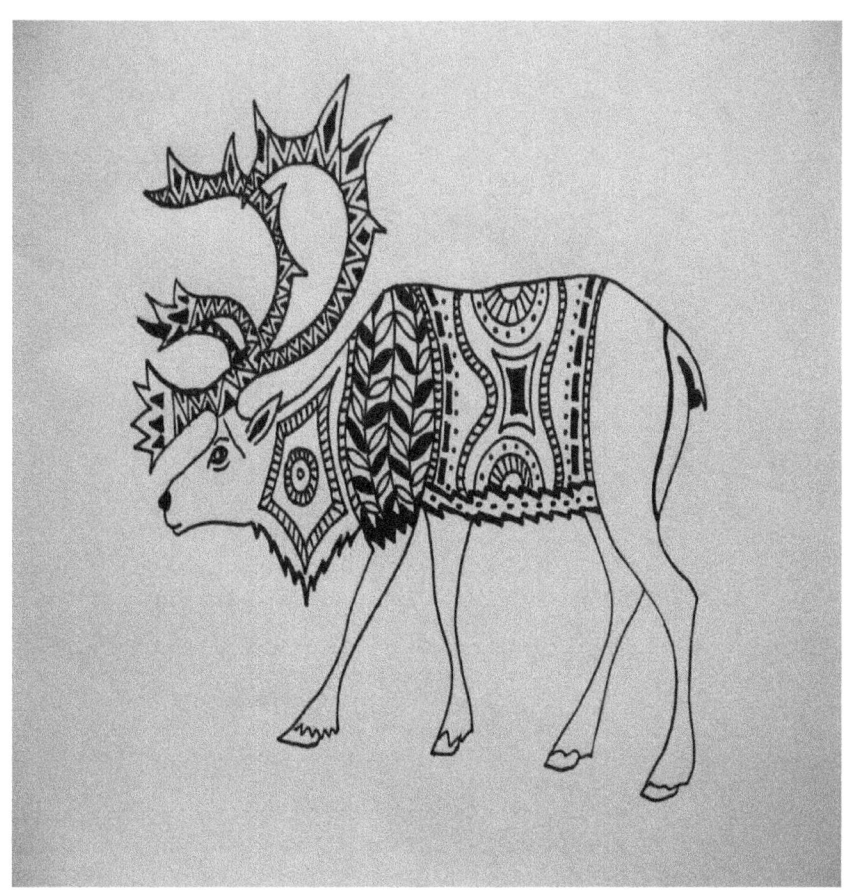

Step 6: You will begin sketching out the shading stamping line under the jaw, the distance down to the mid-section.

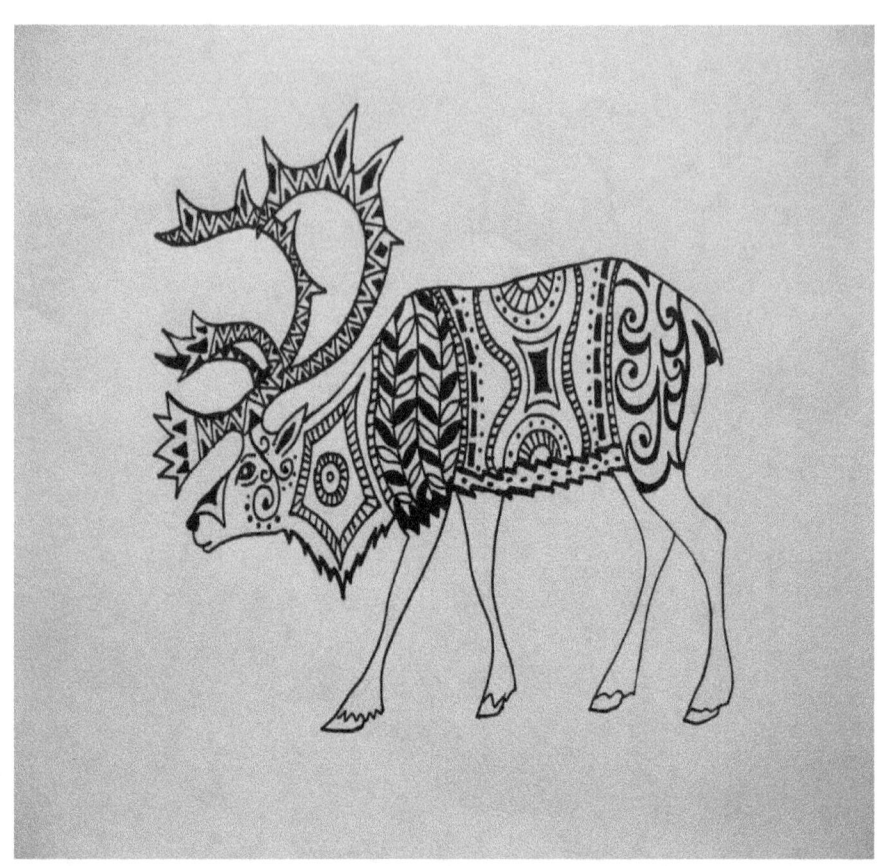

Step 7: Keep on sketching out the state of the soft looking mid-section, and after that draw the states of the reindeer legs and hooves.

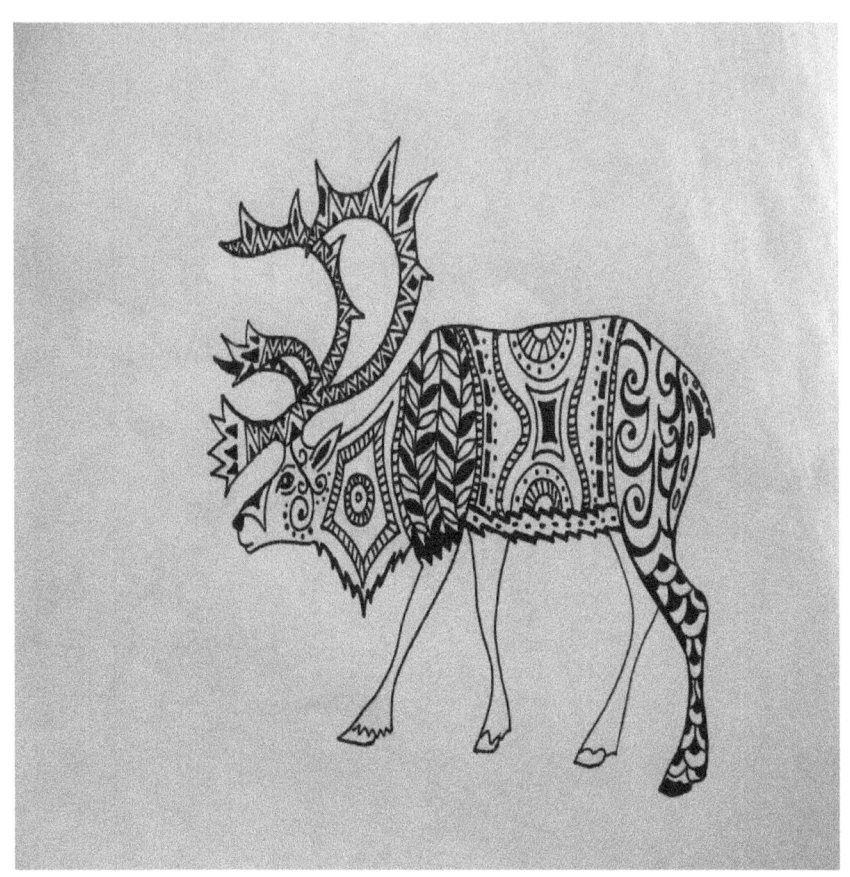

Step 8: Completion draw the from reindeer legs and after that sketch out the state of the paunch under.

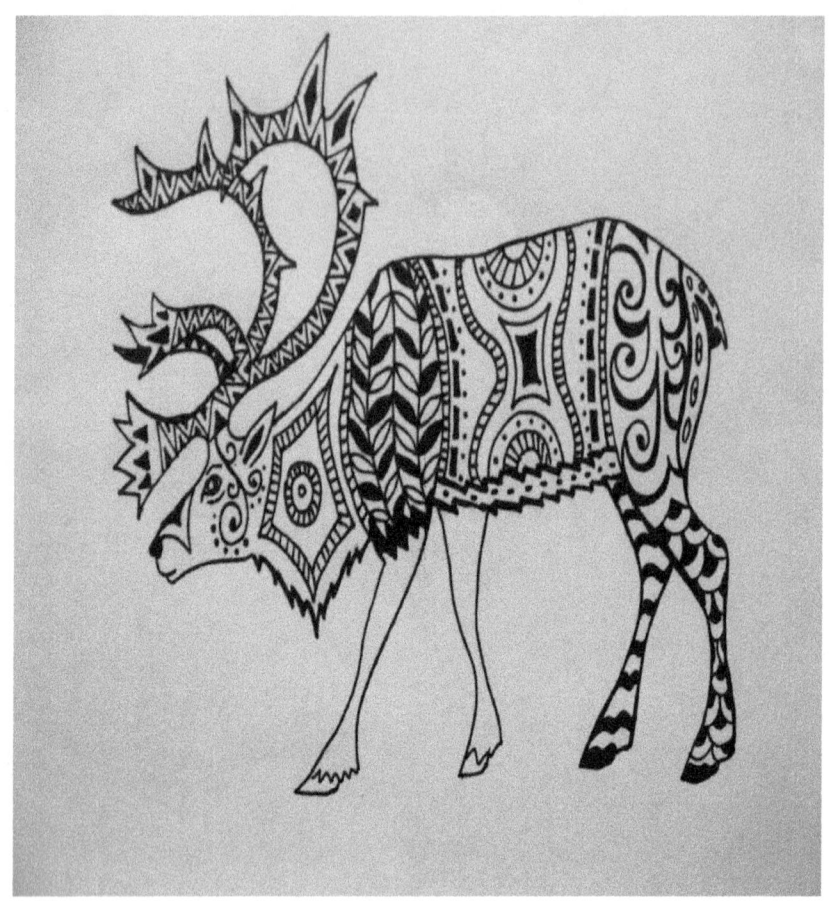

Step 9: In conclusion, draw the starting state of the rear legs and hooves before moving to the following step.

Step 10: For your last drawing step you will draw the state of the back line, and after that sketch out the erect tail, and whatever is left of the rear leg. Delete every one of the rules you attracted step one.

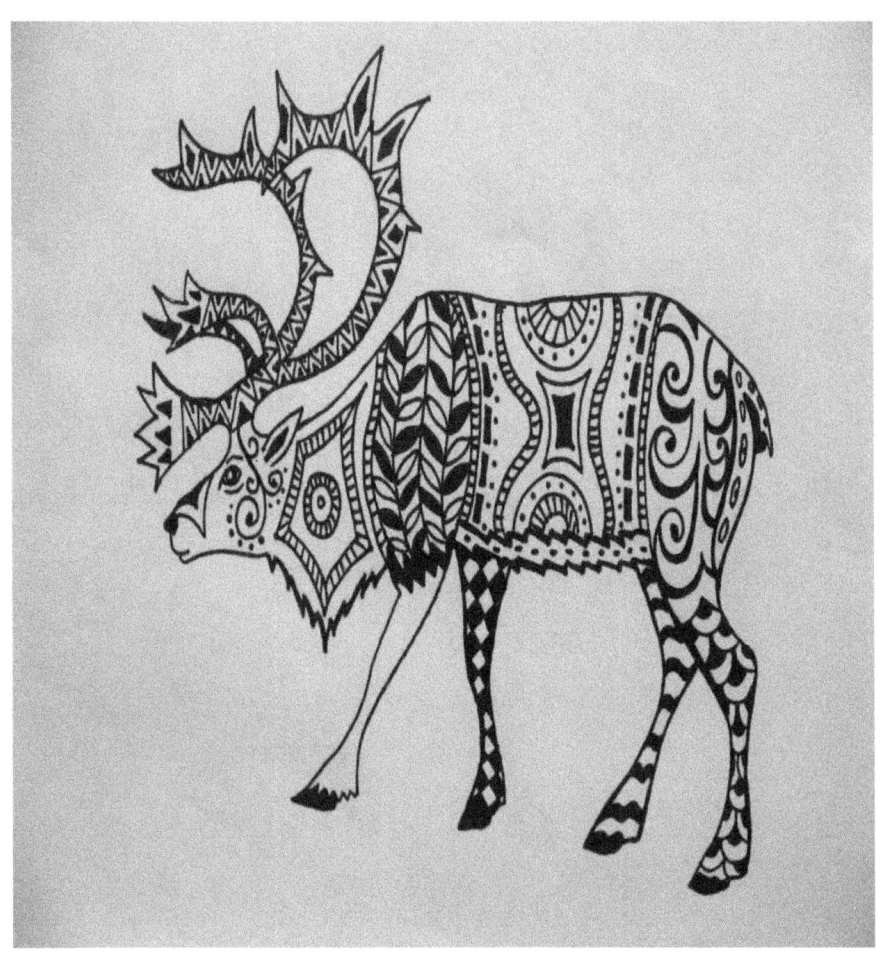

Step 11: This is the means by which you're drawing ought to look when you are finished.

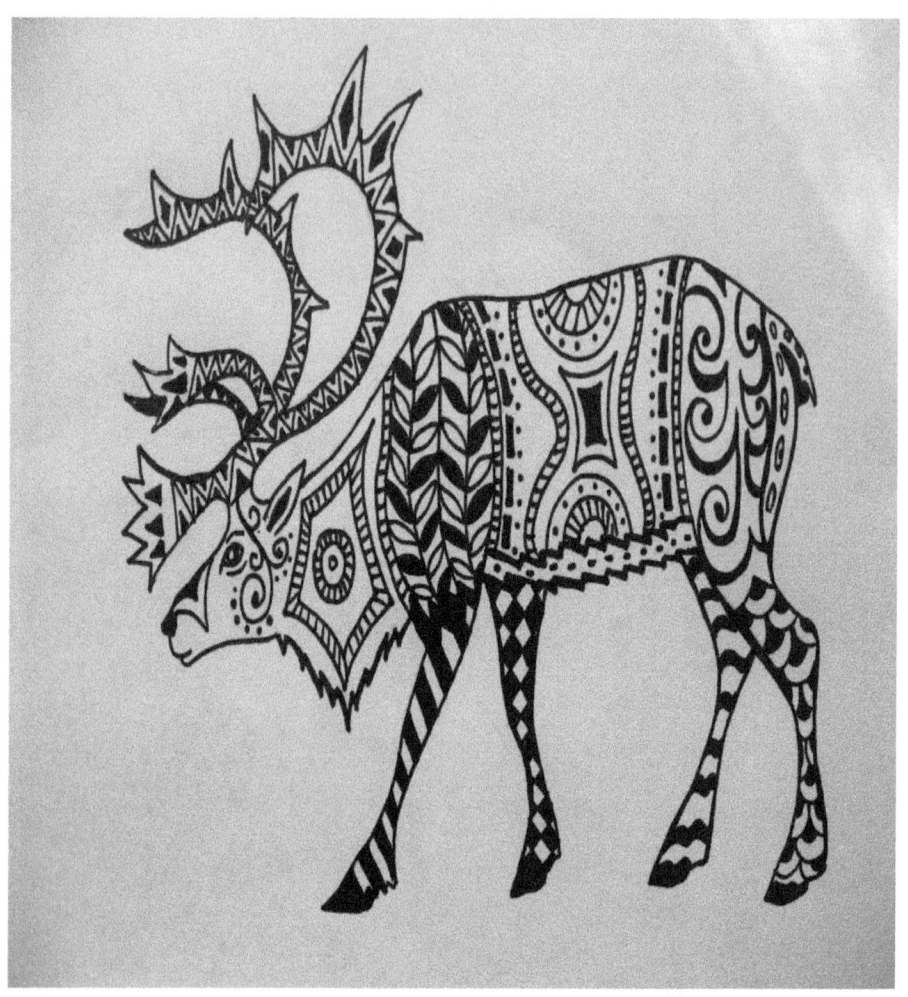

Step 12: Shading in your stormy creature and afterward you are finished with this instructional exercise "on the most proficient method to draw reindeer orderly".

Chapter 6 – How to draw a polar bear

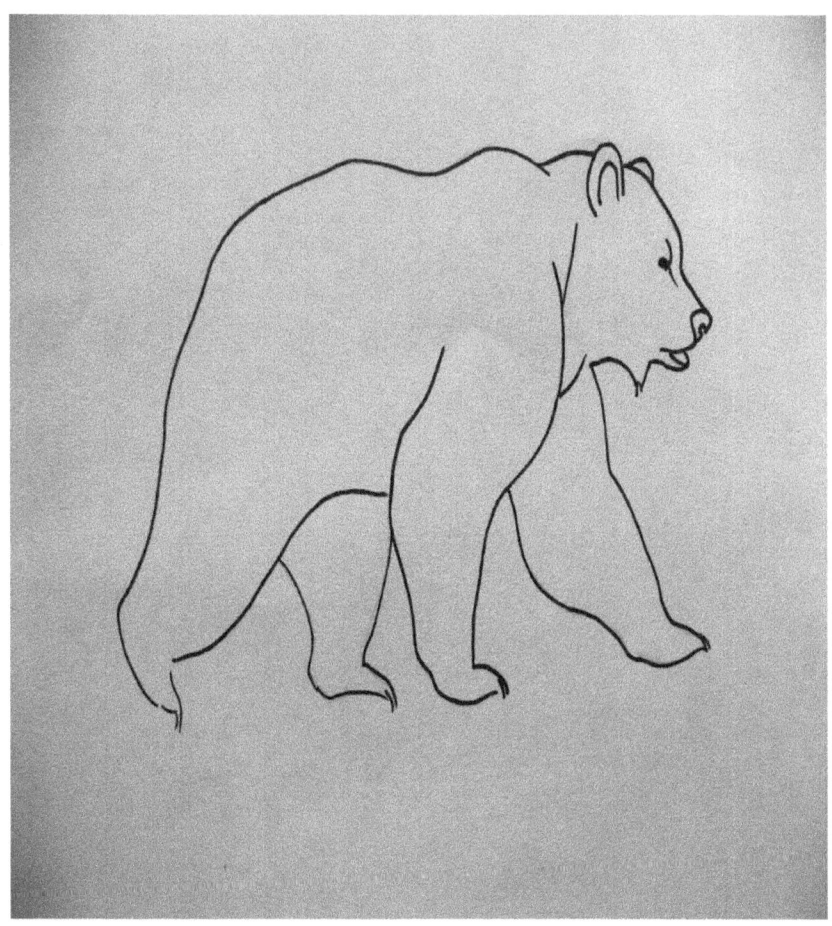

Step 1: Alright first draw an impeccable circle for the head and a not all that immaculate half circle which will be his neck.

Step 2: After that proceed onward by making lines to shape an edge for his body. Simply look at the state of the lines above and duplicate.

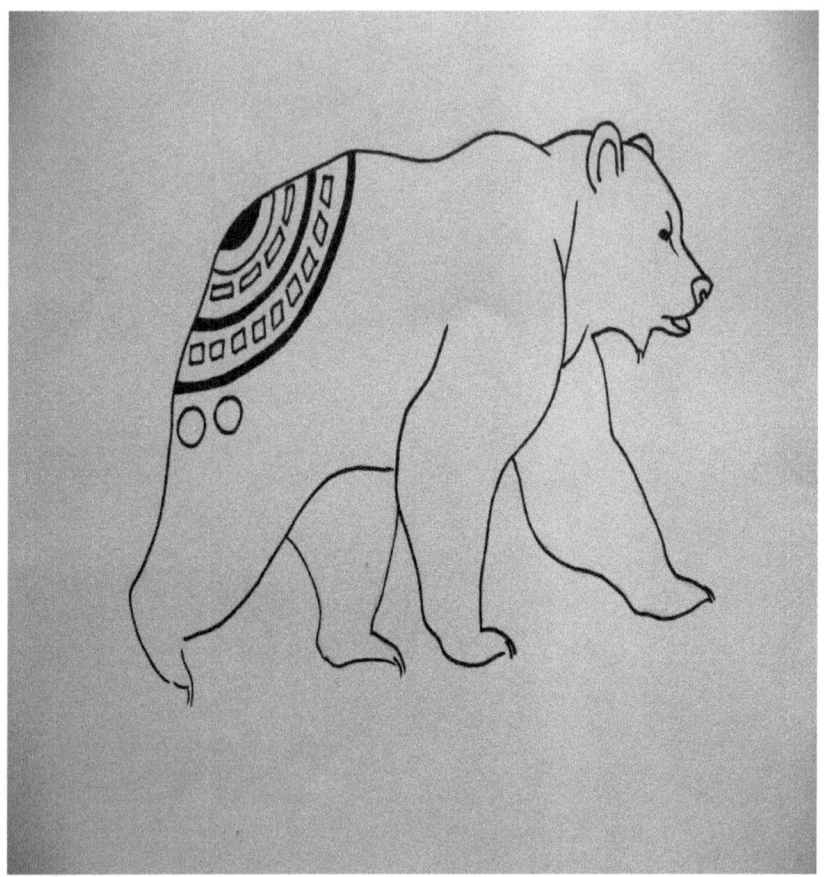

Step 3: As should be obvious it is beginning to take structure. The coating you attracted the past step was the front legs and a portion of the mid-section. What you do here is shape whatever is left of the bears legs and begin to draw his back.

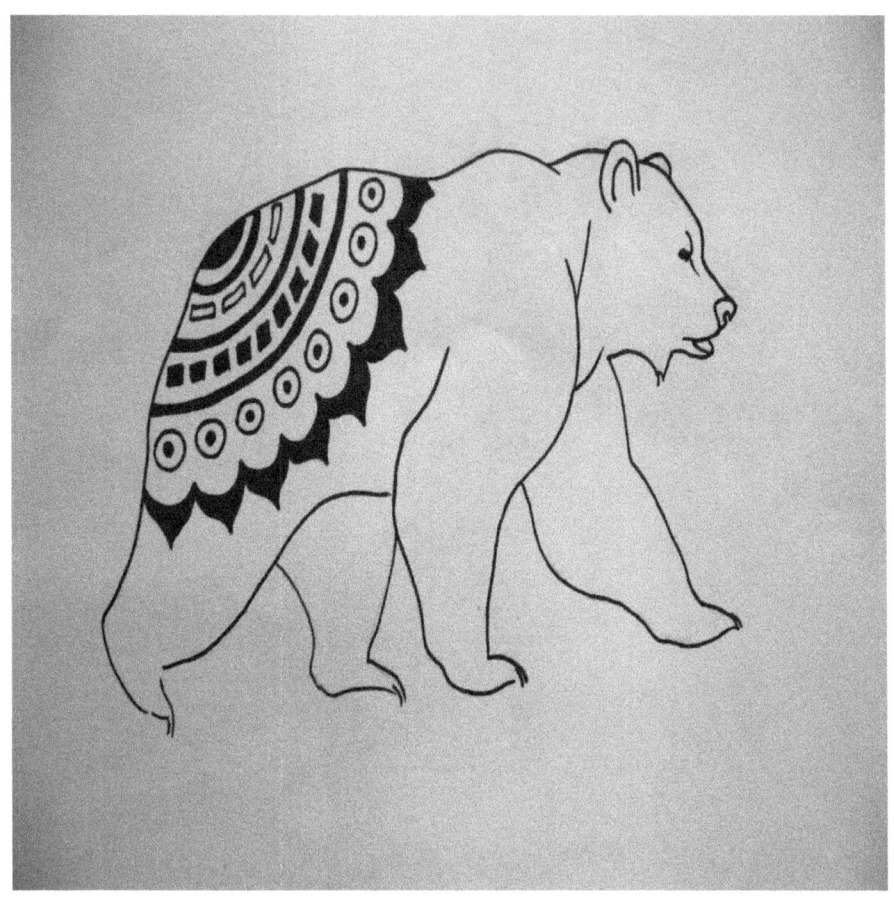

Step 4: Make some minor points of interest in the hide and make the out lines for the toes and rear leg.

Step 5: Presently we can begin chipping away at his face. Draw two little oval circles for the eyes a nose for the nose and a little line for his mouth. Add the nails and also his back lower leg.

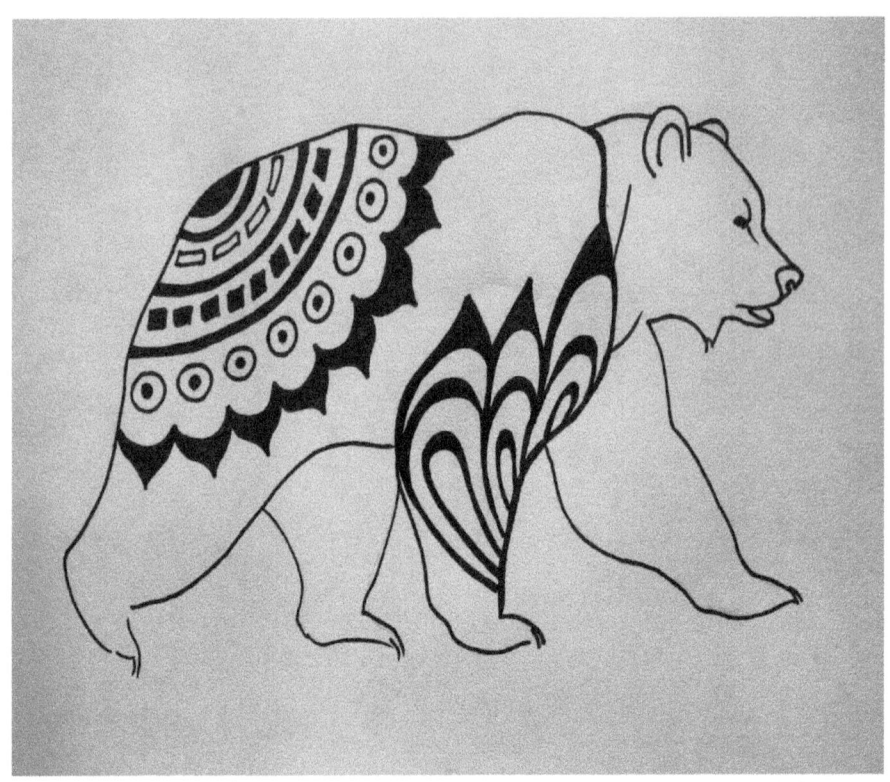

Step 6: Sketch out the ears as appeared and put more detail in the rear foot.

Step 7: Right now the polar bear has taken structure and now is a decent time to begin deleting undesirable lines to tidy up your drawing.

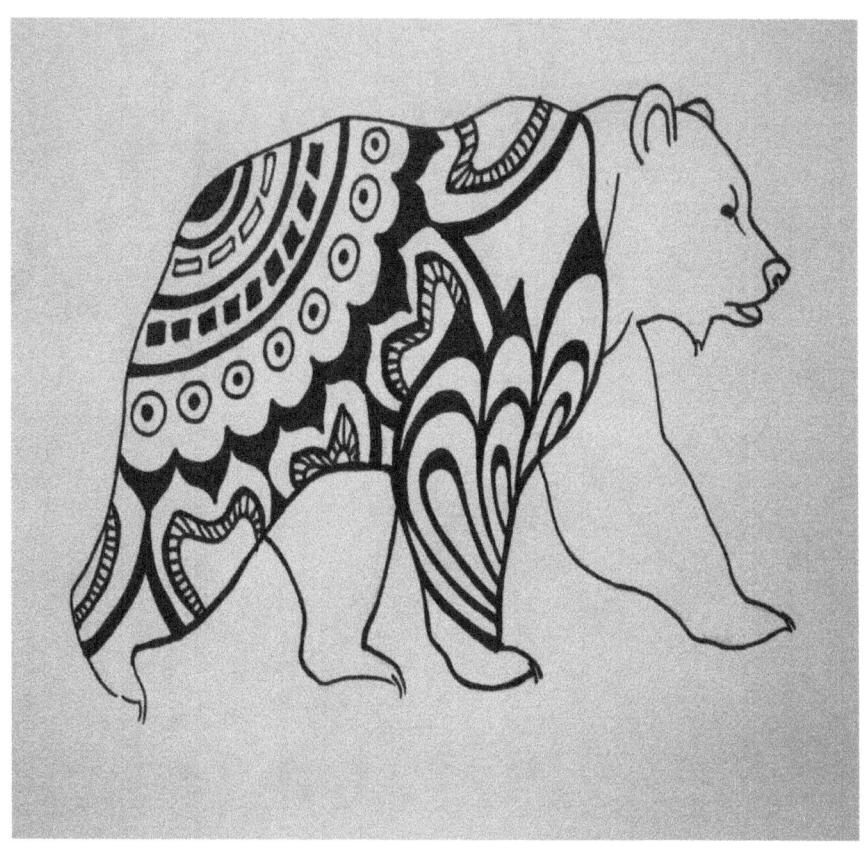

Step 8: Add some puff to his hide and keep in mind make those nails longer and somewhat thicker also. Aftcr that your done your picture ought to like him. Great job

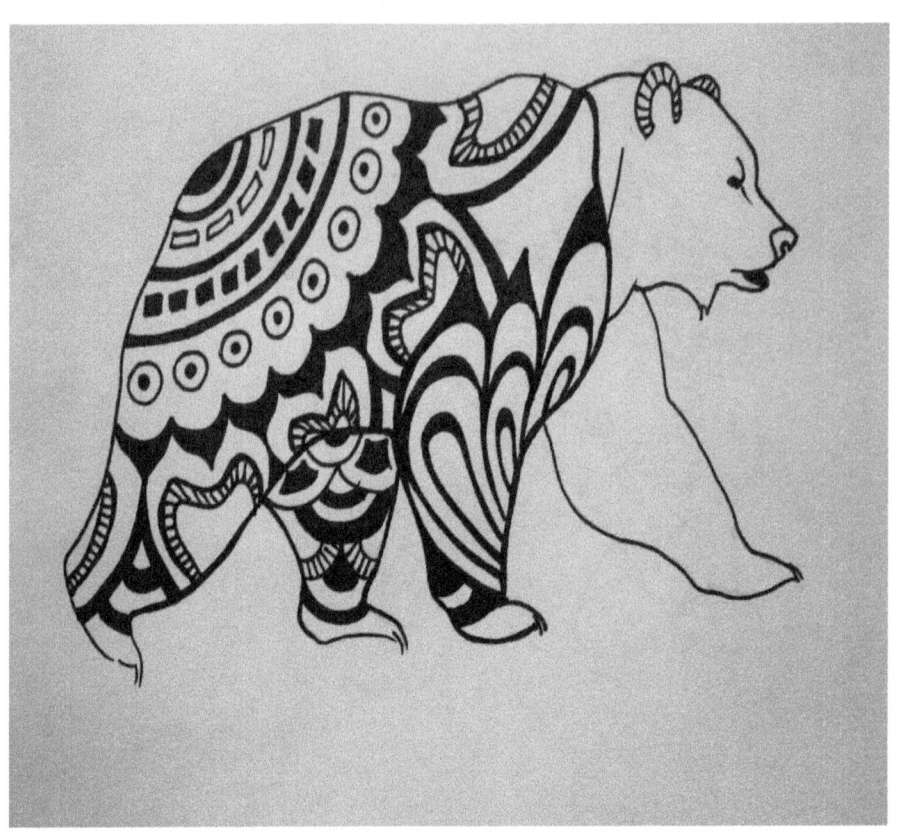

Step 9: Begin this progression by drawing three circle shapes and after that draw the facial rules. These shapes will be the body of the toon polar bear.

Step 10: Presently you will begin drawing out teh charming fluffy face of the bear as you see here. This is an extremely straightforward thing to do in light of the fact that the lines are not as enumerating as a more unpredictable polar bear drawing. When the face is drawing out you can then draw the nose, mouth, and utilized the facial rules to draw out the eyes and students. The exact opposite thing you will do is draw out the state of the legs and feet which incorporates the toes.

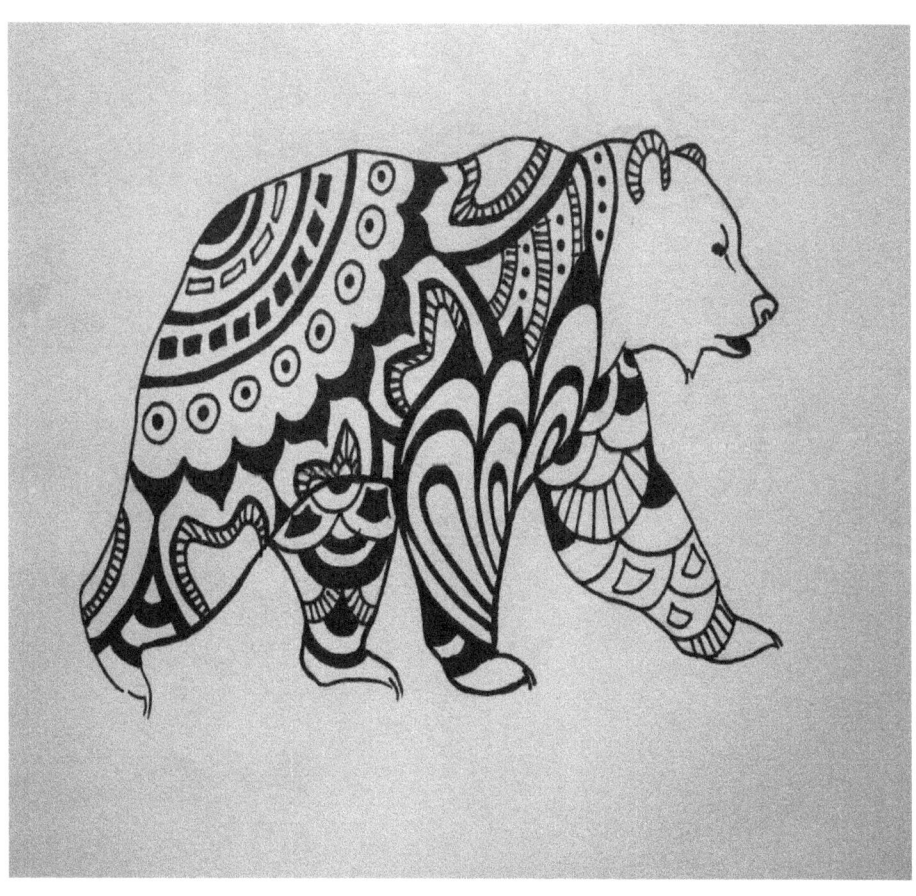

Step 11: Begin this progression by drawing out the state of the polar bears head and after that draw out the ears. You will then sketch out the covering for the extension of the nose. Include nostril openings and after that draw the front external leg and toes. Sketch out the covering of the mid-section and afterward draw out teh back and butt end and tail.

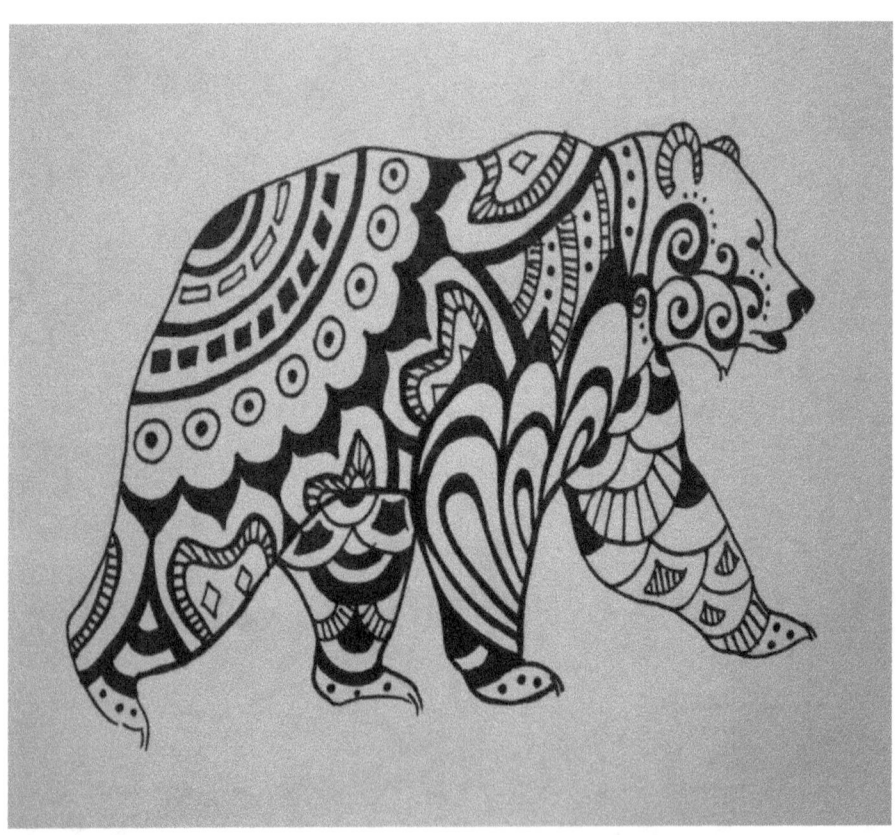

Step 12: Point of interest within the ears and after that include the eyebrows. Complete the process of sketching out the legs and afterward you can begin eradicating every one of the rules and shapes that you attracted step one.

Conclusion

Drawing animals is a standout amongst the most energizing things that your youngsters can learn. As they draw, they can learn a considerable measure. The early phases of drawing will likewise tell you and recognize any gifts that your minimal one may have in the drawing territory.

There are venture to step rules that your tyke can utilize in order to draw animals. As a guardian, you need just the best for your kid and you may take lessons in order to have the capacity to educate your tyke all that you need them to learn. You can likewise take your minimal ones to drawing classes where they can associate with other kids henceforth the learning procedure gets all the more energizing.

At the point when the youngsters are taught how to draw, it turns out to be entirely simple and fun and they can gladly hotshot the splendid work to the folks. For the tyke, self regard is drifted unbelievably. When you need your tyke to draw, there is no requirement for costly manuals. Basic manuals can be viably connected.

The best thing about drawings is the way that one is not required to know how to peruse and compose. This makes it exceptionally proper for minimal ones and it is thoroughly energizing. A youngster or grown-up can learn basic strides of drawing exactly 200 animals in the briefest time conceivable. A youngster is certain to be exceptionally glad when he/she learns to draw something that is unmistakable. A guardian would absolutely feel upbeat to see their minimal one's face light up in energy.

There is a way you can advise that minimal ones adoration to draw. You can see them doodle at whatever point they hold a pen and paper. The minute a kid tries to draw and fizzles, they thoroughly surrender the endeavor particularly when they build up the mentality that they will never have the capacity to do it. Empower the youngster and show him how to make the least complex of drawings. This goes far into boosting the tyke and moving him to activity.

You may consider purchasing one of the many books accessible in the business sector today. They may even astound you by having the capacity to take after the delineated outlines and making mind boggling drawings without anyone else. This should really be possible in the most brief time compass.

The youngster does not have to know how to peruse. Most books will have just representations. The animals are split up into drawings unmistakably demonstrating how one ought to go about each progression of the drawing. Your youngster will really learn a ton from this so don't give them a chance to pass up a great opportunity for the open door.